You're Not Free You're Owned!

By R.W. GLESS

I0428025

DEDICATED

To all the people in America who knew the freedom we had… and to those who will never know the freedom we lost unless they wake up and learn what freedom Our Founding Fathers gave us in the Constitution and Bill of Rights. – *R.W. GLESS*

Table of Content:

ACKNOWLEDGMENTS

I want to acknowledge the Internet. The Internet before the Orwellian socialists took over it and censored the truth. The Internet was once an amazing tool where you could find almost anything... Now those who contributed information throughout the Internet are watched and censored. If they say the wrong thing... they are banned and the information disappears. America has become no better than China or any other controlled Country. And that is a sad epitaph for a one free nation.

Introduction:

"Those who cannot remember the past are condemned to repeat it," - George Santayana.

The USA is half the size of Russia and a bit larger than China but it has enjoyed freedoms those other countries have not, and it has also enjoyed a robust economy. Americans have enjoyed big houses and big cars and freedoms that people in other countries only dreamed of, but those days are gone because America has fallen into a controlled slave state, and it is in steady decline. The future looks grim for America with a bleak job outlook and other economic problems that are only going to get worse. America also had something no other country has had and that was the Constitution. A checks and balance system that allowed the people to weed out and get rid of corruption, and a corrupt government. But the people let their apathy and complacency get the better of them and the corruption now runs unchecked.

Social Fascist Gestapoism had befallen America in the early 2000s in ways that paled The Roman Empire, Nazi Germany, the Soviet Union and even China. The Social Engineers had finally perfected their mind control over the majority by taking over the media. Those who saw through the illusion of freedom and spoke out against the government's plot to slowly enslave the people, were labeled domestic terrorists and publicly denounced as anti-American. Anyone quoting the Constitution had become a threat to the government. FBI and other Government Agencies targeted people who spoke of freedom and liberty. Their message of freedom, and returning America back into a Freer Nation, and demanding the government honor the Constitution and Bill of Rights, was a major threat to the government's supreme power over the people.

What happened in our government was disgraceful. We allowed our elected leaders to boldly lie and we did nothing about it. We stood aside and allow our government to bleed us of our money, personal property, and freedom. We allowed them to inject poison into our food, water and bodies, and we did nothing. Now no one can buy, sell or even live without the mark and permission of the beast called government. America has become a land of the enslaved Sheeple... and what is the biggest amazement is that people don't seem to care or even realize they have been enslaved!

I have written in my last books about the history of our once great nation, and many of you who read it, woke up to see the totally illegal actions our government committed against us.

But most of the people were too afraid to say anything against these crimes. Rule of law had become a joke, and it is the government who is laughing at all of us, because we allowed it to happen! – R.W. Gless

"Fascism is simply a totalizing mobilization of militant, authoritarian and ultra-nationalism forced on everyone... And all private economic enterprise under centralized governmental control.

Socialism is co-operative/collective ownership/management of productive forces forced on everyone, with government in control. Both Fascism and Socialism equal the same thing...slavery!"

$$\sqrt{\frac{Fascism + Complacency}{Apathy + Socialism}}$$

$$=$$

AMERICAN SLAVERY!

Chapter I

America Becomes a Closed Society

The new communist social fascist (CSF) government had finally stripped American citizens of the Right's given them under the Constitution's Bill of Rights. With the stroke of a pen the new Socialist President had taken away the Rights of the people, and now the government could arrest, detain and kill any American without charging them of a crime or allowing them a trial. That dark day was December 31, 2011, when Socialist President Barack Obama signed the National Defense Authorization Act, NDAA, that later was ratified in 2013 when it passed the Senate with a 98-0 vote. That authorization allowed the government the ability to detain citizens indefinitely or kill American Citizens without a trial, eliminating habeas corpus for the American people granted them under the 8 Amendment of the Bill of Rights. Then the Supreme Court Justices, whom were also in league with the Social Fascists, ruled in early 2013 in a case called Salinas v Texas that the 5th Amendment can be used against you in a court of law if you invoke your Right to remain silent. The Justices who don't like Miranda Rights say remaining silent can now be used as an admission of guilt! Freedom from government oppression and Rights that once protected Americans had finally come to an end, and most of the people were oblivious to the horrors that were ahead of them. President Obama also signed a bill HR 347 in 2013 prohibiting free speech, now the Constitution was almost destroyed and those who never spoke out against the tyranny now couldn't speak out at all! The President and his henchmen were also plotting to seize total power over the people. They were hatching a plan that would tell the people that various American States and the leaders of those States were in a "state of insurrection" thus allowing the President to invoke the National Emergencies Act under 50 USC § 1621 and invoke the highly controversial "continuity of government" plan for the United States allowing the President, in essence, to rule with supreme powers and round up all those who defied that power! But would the American people allow it to happen, that was the question?

The Nation Defense Act was also passed that eliminated Habeas Corpus allowing the government to arrest and detain American citizens indefinitely, without a trial, without bail, and without even being charge with a crime!

Questionable acts of deception have been blatantly committed against the people that date back to the late 1700s.

But nowhere near the daily deceptions we see and hear today. We the people do have Constitutional weapons against these deceptions. You just need to know when to use them.

One very important Constitutional Right that we the people have is "Jury Nullification." What is Jury Nullification? Well, it is a tool you have, as a juror that you can use if you find the charge against someone is just plain wrong! So you refuse to convict that person and you vote Not Guilty.

Jury nullification was debated in an 1895 Supreme Court decision, Sparf v. U.S. But as we see today, the Supreme Court played political power games and ruled that judges were not required to tell jurors about jury nullification. The ruling didn't say that jurors didn't have the power or Right to nullify. Nor did it say that judges couldn't tell the jury about nullification; it simply said that the court didn't have to tell the jury they had that power.

This decision has led to the common practice by U.S. judges of penalizing criminal defense lawyers who try to present a nullification argument in front of the jury. Consequently, jury nullification is seen as a de facto power of juries and judges across the country get really pissed off if it is mentioned.

Using Jury Nullification As A Tool To Protect Freedom

If you believe in the Constitution and believe a law like gun control should never be allowed, becoming a stealth juror to get on a jury in order to nullify the law can be beneficial to American Freedom. A smart lawyer will also use a shadow defense to get information entered into the record that would otherwise be inadmissible, hoping that evidence will trigger a jury to nullification. An example of this tactic was the claim by the defense in the Roger Clemens perjury trial to have the charges against Clemens dismissed due to "prosecutorial misconduct", i.e. that the prosecution intentionally introduced video evidence which Judge Reggie Walton had ruled inadmissible, for the purposes of getting, in the words of the defense, "a second bite at the apple", to the jury because of the prosecution's poor performance. The introduction of the tainted evidence caused a mistrial after only two days. The judge denied the defense's motion to dismiss but noted his strong displeasure with the prosecution.

The Government however had fear that nullification could be used to permit violence against socially unpopular factions so they have checks in place. They point to the danger that a jury may choose to convict a defendant who has not broken the letter of the law. However, judges retain the rights both to decide sentences and to disregard juries' guilty verdicts, acting as a check against malicious juries. Jury nullification may also occur in civil suits, in which the verdict is generally a finding of liability or lack of liability (rather than a finding of guilty or not guilty).

But the government is working on a way to avoid possible jury nullifying their wish to convict someone...Trial by judge or arbitrator. If they can push the idea for a long enough time, the sheeple will accept it as law and your chances of winning against the government will be slim and none.

Look at the very conception of the Court. What is a court? A Court is something you play on like a basketball court or a tennis court and in those courts you have a judge or judges, and you hit a ball back and forth and the judge decides who wins. That is what your legal system really is…one big game!

Your Judges wear their black robes as if to say they are your royal master and you know what? That is exactly what the Black Robe signifies the Royal Order of the Garter! A Royal Order that goes back before Christ in pagan times as a worship of Saturn.

*

No man escapes

When freedom fails,

The best men rot in filthy jails;

And they who cried: "Appease, Appease!"

Are hanged by men they tried to please.-

Hiram Mann

Chapter II

As The Screws Turn

Freedom had been under attack for a long time before the 2013 culling of American freedom. Social Engineers had been conditioning the American people's minds for years, dumbing them down to suggestions that government was the answer to all their problems. The term "dumbing down" was thought up in 1933 as a slang word used by motion picture screenplay writers to mean: *"To revise so as to appeal to those of little education or intelligence."* It was quickly adopted by the government as a PR tool, and later used to take further control over the American people.

The dumbing down of America has been a success that is second to no other movement in our history. It has indeed made the citizens stupid. Here is an example of the brain dead people now infesting our once free nation; There is a video on You Tube that shows a man with a SOLID GOLD one ounce Canadian coin, The real Deal, who was trying to sell it for $100 DOLLARS and the people in Southern California in the LA area along the Beach, didn't want to buy this solid gold coin because Canadian money was no good in California.

They actually said that solid gold Canadian money had no value in California. He then asked people if they would pay $50 for the solid gold coin and the people still said Canadian money was worthless in California. This is beyond stupid; it is proof that many of the people have the brains God gave an ice cube. The people/sheeple have been dumbed down in public schools and universities for over 20 years and it sure shows! Stipulations and Regulations have been placed on all Rights granted under the Constitution of the United States. None of the Rights in the Bill of Rights are intact and really haven't been since the great American Civil War.

Since the government has its hands in every aspect of our lives, people are afraid if they speak out against the government, they will be targeted and maybe even fired from their job. America is fast becoming a closed society and bogus arrests are now common and they will start escalating very soon. FEMA camps are very real and will soon be filled up with American Citizens who question the government's authority. If you are unluckily put on the government's Four SSSS list, (Major Security Risk) you will be searched at airports and checkpoints across the nation. And No this isn't a joke, if you see four SSSS on your flight ticket that means you are considered a threat to the government's supreme authority. Finding a job will become harder, especially if you need a background check. You may even be black listed from online sales sites and not allowed to sell on those sites, furthering your inability to make money! The government will do whatever it has to do to frighten you into submission or to ruin you financially so you can't cause them any problems. Then the bogus arrests will begin and the media discrediting you will then start to make you look guilty in the eyes of the people. Since you have no money to fight the government... they win and you lose, rotting in some federal dungeon.

I know this sounds a lot like a nightmare out of some story about Nazi Germany, China or the Soviet Union, but it is happening now as you read this. You can now be arrested in America for being a terrorist and jailed for 10 years for merely protesting, and if you resist, you can be charged with treason and possibly put to death! This is NO JOKE! Any use of force against the government is a crime punishable by death without even a trial if the government deems it necessary.

America has slowly become a prison, and for those who see through the illusion of freedom and try to inform the people of the truth, it will become a nightmare. The First Amendment of the Bill of Rights had finally been abridged when Socialist President Obama sign bill HR 347 into law in 2013, which makes it a felony to protest if the government says you can't because they don't like what you have to say! Corporations now have total control over the media, the press and the people's government. Insurance corporations ruled the day and also rule the American people and Politicians. The people's elected leaders have passed laws that forced Americans to buy health insurance from private corporations. The once free people of America had become subjects over night and the property of a tyrannical Government.

Like livestock on a gigantic ranch, the majority of the people whinnied and bayed in apathetic complacency like the sheep they once herded, stripped of their will to be free. They had allowed themselves to be owned by a master that saw them as nothing more than revenue generating animals. Those who spoke out against the tyranny were labeled crazy people that should not be listened to. Most of the people knew those who spoke out were doing it because they knew allowing the government the power to force people to buy anything was a direct violation of the Constitution… and they were right. But the US Supreme Court had been infiltrated, poisoned and corrupted by the corporate government shills and they ruled that the government now had the power to command the people to obey and buy insurance, or whatever the government deemed was in the best interest of the Country. The Supreme Court Justices Rulings were merely Political Opinions and Political Opinions are like a Fart in a windstorm, they blow the same direction as the political wind blows! Resistance was futile, the citizens were to be assimilated, like taking a page out of George Orwell's 1984 novel... the people had become the property of the Federal Government.

For years the government had been disarming the public in anticipation of taking total control with no regard or threat from the Second Amendment, so the people could not resist the enslavement that was coming. Police were turned into military killing machines, killing anyone who refused to obey the government. They killed citizens without question if their government master ordered it, destroying anyone who witnessed it or spoke out against their murderous Gestapo tyranny. America had become a prison camp to those who could not afford the tens of thousands of dollars a person needed to flee to a free country. Citizen's hatred of the country they once loved was growing every time they were subjected to the tyranny of the new American Gestapo. The corporate government controlled media would quickly create propaganda to convince the apathetic complacent masses that the new American military police were heroes. Even when they were caught on video recordings kicking in the doors of innocent men, women, children and killing the family pet and anyone who moved to protect their family members including children... the complacently apathetic people would not do anything to stop the tyranny. But not everyone believed the corporate government controlled media's lies. More and more people were waking up to see the nightmare they helped create by their silence.

The Government and their Police knew the people were starting to fight back. Citizens were posting videos on the Internet that showed Police tyranny, so the government started to seize the people and their recorders, destroying the evidence that clearly showed the treasonous tyrannical crimes the police perpetrated against the people. Then the police would lie and the controlled Media would tell the masses it never happened, and sadly, many of the American Sheeple believed those lies without question, even after seeing proof to the contrary.

The government had also installed an "Internet Kill Switch" that could be used to stop the spread of information the government didn't want people to know. All forms of communication had been taken over by the government and they were listening to everyone, everywhere! The citizens, sadly enough, would be the very reason the government would take total control over the Internet. The Government had a plan to pretend they are backing away from controlling the Internet and spying on everyone, and if they already haven't said anything about it by the time you read this, they soon will. They will publicly announce they are no longer going to allow agencies to spy on Americans and the people will be safe from government eyes on the internet. Then just like so many other staged catastrophic attacks on the people, the country will be attacked by some "Terrorist" threat to your safety. Of course the sheeple will cry "Help Me Master Government" and the government will jump in and tell the mindless dumbed down masses they will be saved. But only at the price of total control over the Internet and their privacy, and sadly most won't mind because they will be saved by the government!

The government knows that one day the people will rise up against their tyranny. They know all too well that the endless lies they told to take your freedom will one day come back to haunt them. They're not too worried though, because they are working on armored suits that would make the police supermen, impervious to small arms weapons fire. Basically being able to walk up to you under fire and kill you without worrying about getting hurt. Without these super suits, smart people know if they are going to get in a gun fight with Gestapo, they need to aim for the head preferably the face or neck area because that is the least protected and best chance of getting a kill shot. But once these suits get perfected, the citizens won't stand a chance against the government and their enslavement will be sealed. The media will tout these supermen suits as great for our military because our brave men and women will be protected from the "Terrorist's" small weapons fire, and most of the mindless masses will say hurrah to the new super-police/military, never thinking beyond the media hype that those suits will be used against them one day.

'Iron Man suit'

Concept suit from the animated video produced by the Army's Research, Development and Engineering Command

Head gear:
Live data feed projected on a see-through display inside the helmet.

Uniform:
Head-to-toe armor would protect the soldier from bullets and sharpnel.

Civil War · World War I · World War II · Vietnam War · Iraq War · Future

Pack essentials:
The prototype should be able to cure minor wounds with inflatable tourniquets. It would also carry an oxygen supply, cooling system and vital-signs sensors.

The suit would be connected with drones and satellite systems.

Pack weight:
Motors in the exoskeleton would allow a soldier to jump and run carrying 100 pounds or more.

It is called the *"Iron Man Tactical Assault Suit"* and the United States military/police will be wearing these in a town near you as soon as the government perfects them. Once they get these gems perfected it will provide the wearer with superhuman abilities like night vision, enhanced strength, and protection from gunfire... and you can kiss any resistance against your government goodbye because resistance will indeed be futile. Unless of course, you can get one for yourself, but I wouldn't bet on that, but I would however bet the farm it will be illegal for citizens to own... any takers?

The government defiantly has a plan in place to disarm America and damn the Constitution and your Rights, and they have several scenarios where the police will bang on the door then bust in telling residents they have to search for weapons. If too much resistance is seen and cops are being shot at or killed the second scenario will be to go house to house with an armored tank or gun truck and demand over a loud speaker that all residents come outside their homes with their hands on their head. Any home that does not comply would be attacked with tear gas, grenades and bullets before Gestapo/Police/Military entered. This would put a scare into the people's resistance in that area and send a message to others by destroying dwellings and hopefully any weapons and supplies of those resisting might have had.

Now if you don't think this is going to happen you are a

fool. The training of the troops is being done subtly and most people never see it happening. But it is happening and it is happening in a major way. Only those willing to kill on demand are to be trained for the American occupation force. Troops from all over the world are being stationed and trained on American soil and taught to wage urban warfare on Americans. They are being trained to *"Take them out when in doubt"* which means if you are a suspected threat, you will be killed without warning.

I was over at an apartment building in Yuba City, California in the summer of 2014 and was witness to a police raid on a fellow who was reported to have a shotgun and apparently threatening to kill himself. I watched as the police came storm trooping in and blocked off all access, which also blocked me from leaving, which I was about to do. Cops came from all sides and told us to get back as they took out their full auto AR15s. There must have been 20 or more of them there for a supposed man with a gun. I had just been over by this apartment and saw kids in the pool and all seemed calm. The parents who had their kids in the pool were told to stay back, and that had some extremely worried. Finally they got the kids out of the pool and a short time later we heard a flash bang grenade go off and several minutes later they came out with the guy in cuffs. What was the most disgusting to me, was when I saw two cops high-fiving each other with their AR15s held high and one said; "This has been a GREAT DAY!" I couldn't help but think to myself "Gestapo" when I heard that.

I know that you Law Enforcers will try and spin what that cop said as meaning it was a great day because no one got hurt...but that is WRONG! All of those people who witnessed it were hurt and worried mentally, and that display of jack booted storm troopers attacking was not the face of a friendly peace officer. I have known and respect Peace Officers, but have nothing but contempt for Law Enforcing Gestapo. A friend of mine was a Peace Officer before the militarization of the police, and do you know what a Great Day for a Peace Officer is? A day when he didn't have to write any tickets or warnings and he didn't have to use his gun, let alone a machine gun and grenades, because that was a day he knew he had been doing his job, keeping the peace. Merely by his presences, walking his beat, meeting and greeting friends, neighbors, business owners and strangers alike, everyone had a peaceful day. Now that is a GOOD DAY for a Peace Officer!

Ever since the Supreme Court in 2005 ruled that police are not Peace Officers and do not have to keep the peaces, they are now Law Enforcers who are there to "Enforce the Law!" They have been turned into storm trooper Gestapo, and you can expect and bet your life raids will take place against all citizens who refuse to obey. It will only be a matter of time before those who are believers in the US Constitution and Freedom will be targeted. The raids will come early in the morning, and the government attackers will even bring their own film crews dressed in body armor and cameras to video the government rounding up the scourge terrorist patriots who would not denounce the Constitution and the Bill of Rights. Acres of bodies will pile up in government dead zones.

The government has places that now store coffin liners and body bags waiting to be used against you. Your Federal Government has ordered one billion dollars worth of these coffin liners and body bags and a billion dollars can buy a lot of them…and for what? A planned attack on us?

How can you survive an attack by government forces? Well You may not, but here are some things you can do…The first thing you need to know about a raid on your home is that they will either come in early in the morning guns waving and screaming at you, in hopes you are woken up confused… Or they will come in force wearing body armor and carrying AR15s or M16s full auto, with stun grenades ready to kill. Then they will secure your block and remove your neighbors, then shut of all your utilities and jam your cell reception and then give you a call and either try and talk you out or wait you out, or just storm the building after using their grenades. Odds are they will either kill you or capture you unless you have a small army helping out.

But it is always a good idea to have either battery back up or a generator that is secured like a generator in your garage you can use. Have water storage and food storage. Have a 2-way radio like a CB or ham radio you can use. Then try and get as much media attention as possible, especially if you are being attacked for publicly denouncing the government for their violations against our Rights. If you do have Cell phone usage, uplink video of the attackers to your Face Book,

Twitter or YouTube site and try and get as much public support as you can. Then pray others will come and help you before the government takes it down.

A neighborhood militia would be an ideal idea to create. Training yourselves in attack scenarios is also a good idea. Attacking an attacking force from behind or flanking them always scares the hell out of them. Just remember once you head down this road there is no going back, it is full steam ahead and damn the torpedoes. Once you hear the enemy being attacked by your allies from behind, or ahead of you if you happen to be the back up force, you have to hit them with everything you have and you will either win the battle or die fighting tyranny like a free human. Now remember this is a worse case scenario, when and if, the government declares war on those people that not only believe in the Constitution, but those of us who have swore an oath to uphold and defend the Constitution.

If or when that dreadful day comes, those too cowardly to fight and are lucky enough to escape the mass culling of Constitutionalists, but not able to escape America, will hide like scared mice in dark dirty places, many to slowly die of hunger and illness. Only those smart enough to escape America before the government stops the exodus will have a chance of surviving. Those who do not, will be rounded up and will be forced to work as they are herded into cities and camps made to toil from dawn to dusk. If you refuse to work you will not be fed, and anyone caught giving you food will be executed for treason! Only the controlling elite will be allowed the pleasures once known to all Americans, food, clean water and drink, comfort, and only those loyalists will be allowed to freely move about. All the rest will be told what to wear, what to eat, what to drink, where they can live, what they can own, and whom they can talk to. Any violation of the rules will bring swift painful punishment! America will become a nightmare prison for those who remembered the freedoms they once had. Does this sound like an over exaggerated nightmare that can never ever happen in America? Well much of it already has!

You wait and see when the government starts rationing food and gas and other essentials, even housing will become a target. They already are rounding up the homeless that decide to camp on supposed public land. The real sad part is this has been planned for decades. Thee Masters knew one day they wouldn't need people, because machines could do the work more efficiently and with no liability. So you need to be culled… Don't laugh, that day is coming. You can carve that into your tombstone and bet you life and soul on that.

In 2114 this was a News Headline; {*ALBUQUERQUE, NM — Outrage has ignited over a helmet-cam video of officers fatally confronting a homeless man, James Boyd at his primitive campsite in the foothills. Video shows the man standing by his meager possessions, surrounded by rifle-toting officers who were citing him for illegally camping without government permission. Officers ultimately tossed a concussion grenade in his face, sicked an attack dog on him, and shot him to death with a flurry of gunfire.*}

Countless recorded video of cops/Gestapo murdering citizens are out on the internet and have been reported in the news for all to see, yet most of the people never bother to view them, or they say to themselves it can never happen to me. Apathetically complacent towards the video and audio evidence that proves beyond any doubt that the person murdered was murdered without any justified reason, people keep standing aside, looking the other way. Most never realize or even think that if you look the other way, without saying a thing against it...you are in a sense, aiding and abetting the police/Gestapo in the senseless murders of your fellow Americans!

Did you know that over 15% of the police are indeed sociopaths and hope they get the chance to kill someone? A study was done and never released to the public that stated;

"Most people who are attracted to law enforcement careers are sociopaths. Completely lacking in conscience, and unable to feel any empathy for fellow human beings, these monsters are given a badge and gun, and the government backing to impose their will on society. For many years we had intensive psychological tests in place to weed-out these undesirables but in the past two decades these tests have largely been replaced with less intensive ones that don't really predict future behavior problems.

One psychologist that developed new tests for the state of Indiana's law enforcement has stated that conventional tests such as the Minnesota Multiphasic Personality Inventory and Millon Clinical Multiaxial Inventory-III that are routinely given to prospective applicants at Fortune 500 companies cannot be given to applicants of law enforcement agencies because too many subjects would register as psychopaths and thus be ineligible for employment.

What we are now seeing appears to indicate that psychological testing is being used to locate and hire sociopathic deviants rather than a tool to screen them out."

The person who wrote this didn't want their name attached in fear of retaliation.

The rest of those hired as cops are bullies who enjoy harming people and being in total command. If you don't believe this you are indeed a fool, because you have bought into the "police are your friend" propaganda, just as countless other enslaved people have throughout history. Those who are hired as Law Enforcers are chosen because they are willing to shoot to kill and many of them enjoy it! You don't believe that? Just try and disarm the police through legislation and see how much resistance, hate and threats you get from them.

Did you know that there are more sociopath narcissistic personalities in government and law enforcement than there are diabetics in America?

Source: http://wearerespectablenegroes.blogspot.com/2013/05

/is-united-states-of-america-sociopathic.html

**

"Apathy"

Lack of interest, enthusiasm, or concern.

"Widespread apathy among students"

Chapter III

Only Thee Elite Will Be Free

Corporations had become too big to fail because they were created like a pyramid scheme backed up by the governments they controlled. Because the corporations need people to buy what they create, and they employ millions of people, and move billions of dollars, they have become like a standing domino in a long line. If one falls, many more will follow along that line, and the government and its leaders would also be at risk of falling, and they aren't going to jeopardize losing the gravy train they controlled. The Government knows the people are the real corporate assets, so the government treats them like cash-cows. People are told through media and social engineering what to think, what to eat, what to wear, where to live, and what to buy and how to live. The Corporations now own the world and the people in it. The only thing stopping them from totally enslaving the American people, are those pesky people with the freedom of the human spirit and the belief in the Constitution and the Bill of Rights. Those people who know things are very wrong in the once free country called America are the real threat to those who want total control. The corporate globalists are working hard to control any resistance caused by those constitutional minded free spirits, with constant corporate media messaging telling the people to obey. Because if the people ever woke up and realized their financial system was just an illusion and merely a tool to control, the government and the corporations which controlled them would collapse. When the corporate controlled government does collapsed, the people will once again have their freedom back. Of course the people will have to work hard to survive because those who were in control will fight and kill to try and regain control, and you can count on invasion from the UN forces to try and regain that control.

America is the only thing standing in the way of a global government and the elite globalists hate it. They literally hate the Constitution and try to destroy is daily. They have attorneys and their paid politicians and judges working on ways to strip Americans of their Civil Rights. Unfortunately, most Americans just stand aside and watch their Rights slip away.

Did you know that the elite globalist are so well insulated from the commoners that the really important elitists bring their own private toilet with them that is installed where ever they are staying? Yes it is true! For instance, The White House is so concerned about the President's security that the veil of secrecy extends over the president's bodily excretions. The special port-a-john captures feces and urine and is flown back to the United States in the event some enterprising foreign intelligence agency conducted a sewage pipe operation designed to trap and examine waste material of our leaders.

Why does the government take such precautions? Because our government conducts operations collecting urine and feces from foreign leaders and the elite to determine their medical conditions and we don't want them checking on our government elite. Intelligence waste collecting operations have been directed against dictators, dignitaries and political leaders in countries where medical conditions of the top political leaders and elite are considered "State Secrets."

The Israeli Mossad has admitted conducted waste collecting operations against Syrian President Hafez Assad when he visited Amman, Jordan in February of 1999 for the funeral of King Hussein. The Mossad and its Jordanian counterparts installed a special toilet in Assad's hotel room that rerouted the waste to a specimen canister. Assad had diabetes and cancer and the waste spying operation was to discover the actual medical condition of Assad so they could plan future events.

Even Soviet President Mikhail Gorbachev's waste was collected when he visited Washington in 1987. The CIA placed a special trap under a sewage tank to collect the Soviet Union leader's bodily waste for analysis.

The CIA has even collected waste samples from Ugandan President-dictator Yoweri Museveni's toilet when he visited Washington.

Now that the elite leaders know this crap, (pun intended) has been going on, many now take along their own pooper-scoopers with them when they travel.

Just think what personal viruses could be created to attack an individual without infecting anyone else if the government has your DNA and Medical information to work with. That's why the Affordable Healthcare law is so scary. Everything about you is shared with the government, and even if you don't believe you are important enough for them to worry about, you just might be too insignificant and consider a disposable liability!

Control by Edict

Laws in the early 2000s were being enacted at an all time high, and the citizens had no say in the making of those laws.

Most of the people were oblivious to the slow but steady tightening of the chains of bondage. The corporate social engineers knew it was easier to control the minds of people if they were in a large herd. So they started corralling them in cities where they could be conditioned to think and act like the masses living along side of them. Without ever really knowing any of their neighbors, they were conditioned through mass media messaging. The people were being programmed like mindless robotic automatons. They had become so stupid many of them didn't even know what the Bill of Rights was! The city dweller had become unlike those people who lived in small communities. Those who live in small towns know their neighbors for miles around. But in the city people don't really know the people who live next door, and could care less about anyone but themselves. People in small towns banned together to protect one and other from threats like thieves and thugs, and talk to each other to find solutions to problems that might arise. People in the city only looked out for themselves and hardly ever looked out for anyone else or talked to their neighbors. The city dwellers are not allowed to find solutions because that is the job of the government, so most don't bother and eventually given up hope that things will change.

The corporate governments knows a divided people are

much easier to control than a united people, so Agenda 21 was implemented to herd people into cities where they will be disarmed and reduced to living in a small space. Their own personal space or cage, free but not really free, because cities have many rules and regulation you have to follow. But this was not enough; they had to control the people's life and needed the ability to control their lives. So they devised a plan to take over the people's healthcare, essentially controlling life, and in the process totally destroy the Constitution so they could take total control over all human life in America!

The thing corporate government hates the most is independence, because they need all humans working to support the government in corporate jobs that pay a wage they can control and tax. Only then can the corporate government know how much money the people make, and how much they can take, and only then would they be able to force them to pay for living in America. In the Cities, people not allowed to own livestock or grow their food. They have to buy everything to survive and that makes the corporate government rich. Every time you buy anything, what extra charge is added into the price? Taxes! Whether it be sales tax or income tax, property tax, there is a tax imposed by the government on what you buy, make, create, consume, even the water you drink and the air you breath is taxed in some way. So the corporate government started passing laws, regulation and taxes, making it hard for people to live in the country and produce their own necessities. The counties, states and federal governments passed restrictive laws and charged excessive fees and taxes on those who wanted to live away from the masses. The government charges outrageous taxes for fire protection and policing protection that is non-existent in many rural areas. Only if the local town's people put together a volunteer fire department or petitioned their state or county to allow the people to elect one of their own as local sheriff or patrolmen, can they get the protection they are forced by law to pay for.

Living in America has become like living under the thumb of the government masters of old in the former Soviet Union, Nazi Germany, and China. Only if your master government gives you permission, can you do what you want with your own land, property and life. This is a sad epitaph for a once free Country, because free men and women shouldn't have to ask for permission from their masters, and free men and women aren't forced by their government to buy anything! Any people who think they are free living in any country that forces the people to obey without question and are forced buy anything, is a country of enslaved fools!

The people now work for the government and those in power have an iron hold on every aspect of human life. They control just about everything, and they are even trying to control the most important thing of all, Water! They can never totally control all the water because of rain and natural streams and rivers, but they are trying, and have a hold on man made lakes and reservoirs and charge for the water they control. The government is even passing laws to control the ground water and the wells that people own. The President of the United States, Barack Obama, even tried to close the oceans at one point so no citizen could use them. Once the people allowed the corporate government control over all water, all freedom will be controlled and there won't be any freedom at all... America's enslavement will be total and final!

There are still free places to go in the early 2000s, but the American government makes it very hard to escape America. If you attempt to leave America and take your money with you, beware, because the Government frowns on their property (YOU) trying to escape! They will tax away your money and hound you for more tax if you escape to a country America has control over. So you need to find a country that doesn't allow America to control it. People fleeing America had already overwhelmed Canadian Authorities in the early

2000s. Americans were Illegally Immigrating to Canada because it was easier to take their money there, and leave from there to other freer destinations. There were many also leaving to Mexico and South America as well. So the American government made it mandatory to have a passport to visit Canada and Mexico. Years ago you didn't need a passport to go into Mexico or into Canada, but that had to be changed to stop the exodus of Americans and the influx of illegal aliens who don't pay any taxes.

The Government did a study on Americas living outside the USA and found that 6.4 million people were no longer living and working in America. Almost all of them had moved to countries that had far more personal freedom than America and many of those people would become citizens of their new country. The numbers of American people living abroad had skyrocketed in a 2-year period from 1% to well over 5% and the trend was also skyrocketing with American from ages 25 to 35 thinking of leaving the country. Ages 18 to 40 had shown a major increase in a 4-year period from 15% to 40% that would like to have another home in a different country. This was a valid study and not fiction folks. Needless to say, it was a scary trend for the government and they had to figure out a way to put a stop to it.

So the Federal Government is working on passing laws that would forbid any American Citizen from fleeing the country if they owe taxes, fines, and student loans or have any American debt at all. Passports will be revoked, and if caught trying to escape America, you will be arrested and convicted then sent to a FEMA detention/re-education center forced to work off your debt to the corporate government. If you are lucky enough to be able to escape from behind the American Iron Curtin, countries like Croatia, Kazakhstan, Bhutan, Dubai, Western Sahara, Brazil, Paraguay and Uruguay are safe havens but have less over all freedom. They just won't allow America to demand they return you to America. At least for now.

Many of the countries in South America are also freer than America in many ways and could be a safe place but you need to check out their laws and if they cooperate with American demands. Brazil is one of those Country the American Corporate Government does not want the American people to know about because Brazilians cannot be extradited to any country period, it is in their Constitution, and you can become a Brazilian Citizen in as little as 12 months. Brazil also does not allow America's rogue agencies like the IRS to seize the assets of Americans, or former Americans, who move there to escape the American tyranny. Brazil also voted into their

Constitution in 2005 that they have the Right to own guns. Best choice is Uruguay if you are basically white since they have the highest level of whites living there and you can blend in easier than most of the other South American countries. Some of the American controlled South American countries will likely kick out American patriots if the American Government demands those countries return former American citizens. So you have to choose carefully and make sure you can survive there, making some kind of a living if you don't have enough money to live on. Sadly the American media propaganda machine keeps most Americans obvious to countries like Brazil, Uruguay, Paraguay, Croatia, Kazakhstan, Bhutan, Dubai, Western Sahara, because most have no extradition treaty with America. Sadly if the Global Masters get their way…nowhere will be free.

Now the freest Nation according to many studies, and the only other country that believes you have the Right to Bear Arms other than America and Brazil, is New Zealand, but they have pre-70s American laws on abortion. So by many who study over all freedom, New Zealand is the number one freest nation on the planet. But they don't just let in anyone. You have to be either a professional or well off money wise to get into New Zealand. America has fallen well below the top ten in over all freedom and it was rated 47th when it comes to freedom of speech. The Netherlands, Hong Kong, Australia, Canada, Ireland, and even Cambodia, yes Cambodia, finished above the U.S. in over all freedom other then the right to bear arms.

Now you're going to hear the ludicrous sheeple tell you that if you leave America and give up your citizenship you can never come back, and to those who tell that to you.... you have to do a belly laugh. Because thousands of illegal aliens enter the USA every day and most are never caught or deported! So once you leave and find a country you like, if it doesn't work out, well hell, while you are looking for a new one you can come back to the USA and live without having to pay taxes or worry about money because the government will give you Alien Assistance Welfare and you'll never have to worry about being deported as long as you move around.... Hell you'll have all the free-bees and none of the enslaving payments and taxes American citizens have to pay. Yes, I know, you never though about that before now, have you?

It is also laughable that Americans think they have freedom and protection from their abusive government because of the Constitution and Bill of Rights, because in reality they have no protection at all. Police and Judges have no use for the Constitution or the Bill of Rights and routinely tell anyone who invokes those documents that they are out of order and if they mention their Rights again they will be held in contempt of court, or if they are confronting Gestapo they are arrested for P.O.P. pissing off police! Sadly, the majority of the people in America now cower in fear and allow themselves to be abused. Literally soiling their pants when police grab them and tell them they are under arrest for some bogus charge. All because they stood their ground and asked what authority the Gestapo had to threaten and arrest them. After their arrest they cower in jail and are threaten with long prison time if they don't cop a plea to a crime they never committed. But this isn't the most outrageous of the crimes the government commits against the people, not by a long shot. The Courts will demand the jury convict you if you dare challenge them by taking it to court, and expose the government abuse in public. Many of the Judges in America will come down hard on anyone who dares to expose the government's corruption and shows the people that the government creates crimes to convict you if you dare question their authority!

This really happened in a little known case in a little known town in northern California in the County of Yuba, where two young men (Brothers) were arrested and convicted for protesting taxes. Video was live-streamed to YouTube and shows the two young men were merely holding a sign on an overpass in Yuba County that said; "Taxes=Theft" when swarms of Sheriff and California CHP/Gestapo surrounded and interrogated them. They had several Gestapo searching for a reason to arrest these two and finally came up with a bogus law that had nothing to do with protesting. It was later was dropped by the Yuba County District Attorney, but other bogus charges were filed against them by the District Attorney who later ran again for the job and won unchallenged! But the publicity live streamed video of the arrest that was recorded at the time, seen on YouTube, created a lot of interest and the two men were on radio talk shows after that video went viral. No one anywhere thought a jury could convict these two, but the district attorneys searched and searched for some way to convict them and create a legal precedence allowing them to arrest any protesters, or anyone, and they found it; Detaining an Officer in the performance of their duties. Yep, they charged and convicted the two young men because the Sheriff and CHP had to confront and harass the two protesters.

This clearly shows you have no Rights in America anymore and you can and will be arrested for P.O.P. if you piss off police. The Jury was not allowed to view the entire video and was basically told they had to convict these young men, and they did. The Jurors were oblivious to the real case at hand, the ability to protect grevences and the First Amendment. The Judge told the Jury the charges had nothing to do with the First Amendment and the jury just bahed along like good little sheeple without so much as the brains God gave an ice cube and convicted these two. The Jury litterally allowed the government to set a precedent to arrest people for utilizing their Rights clearly stated in the Bill of Rights. At their sentencing their father who was at the time a Major in the USAF read a speech questioning what he was fighting for in America and stating his sons were doing more for freedom than he had in his whole time with the military. It was a speech reminiscent to Patrick Henery's Give me Liberty or Death and after he was done reading it, I applauded and was promptly thrown out of the Courtroom for my out burst of public courtroom disobedience. No longer can anyone in a courtroom move, speakout, talk, motion, nod, applaud or even wipe a runny nose without getting thrown out. Justice in America has become a joke complete with little tin-gods that rule as if they are your supreme god. No more "order in the court" spouted by the judge, just 4 or 5 bailiffs with guns and tasers running over and forcefully removing the people who protest. So the legal system has created a fear into the people, and basically are telling the people they can't do anything about abuses against the Constitution and Bill of Rights that the Judge will commit. The words "Blind Justice" now take on a whole new meaning in America.

The Police and the Government are now above the law and will tell the citizens they are exempt from the laws that the people have to obey. The people have allowed them to become the controlling elite and "You" have become slaves of the state and there is nothing short of revolution or a wakening revolation that is going to free the people. America's government has moved quickly to strip the citizens of freedom. They are trying to imposed a Constitution Free Zone 100 miles wide around the country. This would give them the ability to use whatever tactics needed to stop people from leaving or entering the USA.

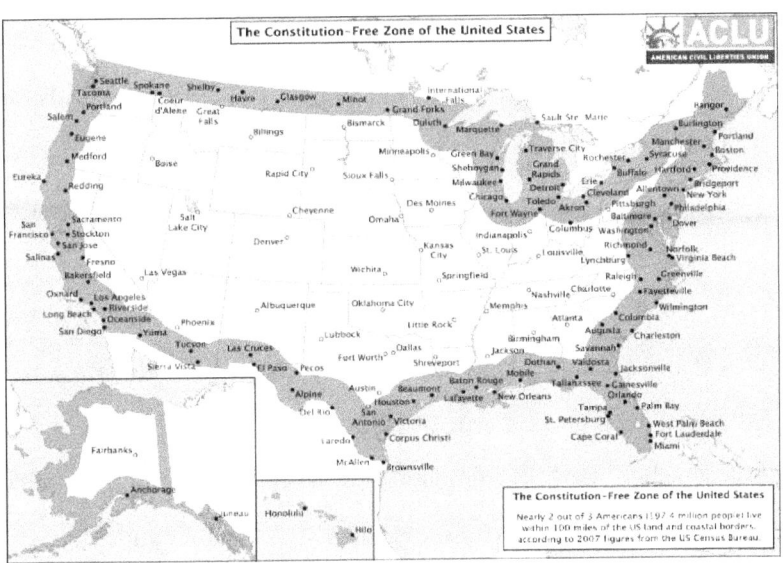

45

This is the Constitution Void Zone and You can be searched and detained without a warrant in these zones if we allow the government to get away with it.

It is only a matter of time before all the freedom Americans had, will be gone forever, and most of the people are oblivious to the enslavement they are under. What makes this even more unbelievable is that most Americans are apathetically complacent about it! The word "Sheeple" is right on, because it is like looking into the eyes and face of a Sheep. I don't know if any of you have ever done it, but to me and many people who have, the blank look that a sheep has, makes it look like one of the stupidest creatures there is. Then again maybe the Sheep are thinking the same thing about Humans?

The Government had been dumbing down children for so long, decades in their schools, and the government is never going to educate the people on how to stop the tyranny the government is committing against them. Only those older Americans who knew that the Constitution and Bill of Rights was once the law of the land, have a chance of educating the young, but it was hard to convince those who had been brainwashed that the Constitution and Bill of Rights were worth saving. Most of the citizens have no conception of their granted freedom and the controling elitest government isn't going to tell them about it.

It never ceases to amaze me when I read that someone in government has an intellectual solution to the haves and have-nots. They guarantee if they pass a law the people will see miraculous results, but first they have to pass it. My amazement is the fact that their vanity assumes their solution is backed up by some study or statistics gleaned from questions created by themselves, when is reality it is to control the people.

One very important fact is always missing in their divine revelations. We live in a parasitic universe, and everything feeds off of something else, thus survival of the fittest. Therefore there is always going to be the haves and have-nots. The best thing we can do is just make sure no one is being physically hurt or threaten and let people have the freedom to choose their own destiny.

There are only 2 constants in our dimensional universe; #1: Nothing lasts or lives forever. And therefore #2 Everything dies. I have had some people try and inject a 3rd "Being Created" but that is an irrelevant since we are here and if we were not here, nothing would be a constant or matter period. So to think man can ever achieve some utopian Shangri-La of equality is merely an illusion. Man is a parasitic animal whether it wants to believe that or not, and therefore there will always be those who succeed and those who do not. You can take as much as you want from those who have and give it to those who have not, but those who have will eventually find a way to stop that. That is just how it is, so educating the down trodden and not conditioning them to expect a free ride, is the answer to helping them achieve self sufficiency and a livable existence.

***

"Complacency"

A feeling of quiet pleasure or security,

Often while refusing to see, or
unaware of potential danger, defect, or

pending doom.

Self-satisfaction or smug satisfaction with an
existing situation, condition, etc.

"The people were complacent and failed to act when the
government took their freedom from them."

Chapter IV

Destruction of the Bill of Rights

I am going to show how the first ten amendments in the Bill of Rights have been basically shredded. As a matter of fact we really have no Bill of Rights anymore because the courts ignore it for the most part unless there is public outrage.

These are your Rights that you should never allow to be taken or changed into a privilege, but if you don't speak up and say no to the degeneration, they will be totally gone soon! Many of your Rights have already been converted into privileges and it is because not enough people spoke up to stop it.

Our founding fathers adopted the philosophy of the age of enlightenment and age of reason. This philosophy was a collective idea by Francis Bacon (1562-1626), Baruch Spinoza (1632–1677), John Locke (1632–1704), Pierre Bayle (1647–1706), Voltaire (1694–1778), Francis Hutcheson, (1694–1746), David Hume (1711–1776) and physicist Isaac Newton (1643–1727). The reason I am telling you about this is because our Constitution was conceived around this philosophy. John Locke's ideal that "All Men Have Inalienable Rights" was incorporated into the U.S.

Constitution.

Now I want to show you what the Founding Father George Mason had written which was the basis of the Bill of Rights:

Amendments Proposed by the Virginia Convention June 27, 1788

That there be a Declaration or Bill of Rights asserting and securing from encroachment the essential and unalienable Rights of the People in some such manner as the following;

First, That there are certain natural rights of which men, when they form a social compact cannot deprive or divest their posterity, among which are the enjoyment of life and liberty, with the means of acquiring, possessing and protecting property, and pursuing and obtaining happiness and safety.

Second. That all power is naturally vested in and consequently derived from the people; that Magistrates, therefore, are their trustees and agents and at all times amenable to them.

Third, That Government ought to be instituted for the common benefit, protection and security of the People; and that the doctrine of non-resistance against arbitrary power and oppression is absurd slavish, and destructive of the good and happiness of mankind.

Fourth, That no man or set of Men are entitled to exclusive or seperate [sic] public emoluments or privileges from the community, but in Consideration of public services; which not being descendible, neither ought the offices of Magistrate, Legislator or Judge, or any other public office to be hereditary.

Fifth, That the legislative, executive, and judiciary powers of Government should be seperate and distinct, and that the members of the two first may be restrained from oppression by feeling and participating the public burthens, they should, at fixt periods be reduced to a private station, return into the mass of the people; and the vacancies be supplied by certain and regular elections; in which all or any part of the former members to be eligible or ineligible, as the rules of the Constitution of Government, and the laws shall direct.

Sixth, That elections of representatives in the legislature ought to be free and frequent, and all men having sufficient evidence of permanent common interest with and attachment to the Community ought to have the right of suffrage: and no aid, charge, tax or fee can be set, rated, or levied upon the people without their own consent, or that of their representatives so elected, nor can they be bound by any law to which they have not in like manner assented for the public good.

Seventh, That all power of suspending laws or the execution of laws by any authority, without the consent of the representatives of the people in the legislature is injurious to their rights, and ought not to be exercised.

Eighth, That in all capital and criminal prosecutions, a man hath a right to demand the cause and nature of his accusation, to be confronted with the accusers and witnesses, to call for evidence and be allowed counsel in his favor, and to a fair and speedy trial by an impartial Jury of his vicinage, without whose unanimous consent he cannot be found guilty, (except in the government of the land and naval forces) nor can he be compelled to give evidence against himself.

Ninth. That no freeman ought to be taken, imprisoned, or disseised of his freehold, liberties, privileges or franchises, or outlawed or exiled, or in any manner destroyed or deprived of his life, liberty or property but by the law of the land.

Tenth. That every freeman restrained of his liberty is entitled to a remedy to enquire into the lawfulness thereof, and to remove the same, if unlawful, and that such remedy ought not to be denied nor delayed.

Eleventh. That in controversies respecting property, and in suits between man and man, the ancient trial by Jury is one of the greatest Securities to the rights of the people, and ought to remain sacred and inviolable.

Twelfth. That every freeman ought to find a certain remedy by recourse to the laws for all injuries and wrongs he may receive in his person, property or character. He ought to obtain right and justice freely without sale, compleatly and without denial, promptly and without delay, and that all establishments or regulations contravening these rights, are oppressive and unjust.

Thirteenth, That excessive Bail ought not be required, nor excessive fines imposed, nor cruel and unusual punishments inflicted.

Fourteenth, That every freeman has a right to be secure from all unreasonable searches and seizures of his person, his papers and his property; all warrants, therefore, to search suspected places, or sieze any freeman, his papers or property, without information upon Oath (or affirmation of a person religiously scrupulous of taking an oath) of legal and sufficient cause, are grievous and oppressive; and all general Warrants to search suspected places, or to apprehend any suspected person, without specially naming or describing the place or person, are dangerous and ought not to be granted.

Fifteenth, That the people have a right peaceably to assemble together to consult for the common good, or to instruct their Representatives; and that every freeman has a right to petition or apply to the legislature for redress of grievances.

Sixteenth, That the people have a right to freedom of speech, and of writing and publishing their Sentiments; but the freedom of the press is one of the greatest bulwarks of liberty and ought not to be violated.

Seventeenth, That the people have a right to keep and bear arms; that a well regulated Militia composed of the body of the people trained to arms is the proper, natural and safe defence of a free State. That standing armies in time of peace are dangerous to liberty, and therefore ought to be avoided, as far as the circumstances and protection of the

Community will admit; and that in all cases the military should be under strict subordination to and governed by the Civil power.

Eighteenth, That no Soldier in time of peace ought to be quartered in any house without the consent of the owner, and in time of war in such manner only as the laws direct.

Nineteenth, That any person religiously scrupulous of bearing arms ought to be exempted upon payment of an equivalent to employ another to bear arms in his stead.

Twentieth, That religion or the duty which we owe to our Creator, and the manner of discharging it can be directed only by reason and conviction, not by force or violence, and therefore all men have an equal, natural and unalienable right to the free exercise of religion according to the dictates of conscience, and that no particular religious sect or society ought to be favored or established by Law in preference to others.

AMENDMENTS TO THE BODY OF THE CONSTITUTION

First, That each State in the Union shall respectively retain every power, jurisdiction and right which is not by this Constitution delegated to the Congress of the United States or to the departments of the Foederal Government.

Second, That there shall be one representative for every thirty thousand, according to the Enumeration or Census mentioned in the Constitution, until the whole number of representatives amounts to two hundred; after which that number shall be continued or en-creased as the Congress shall direct, upon the principles fixed by the Constitution by apportioning the Representatives of each State to some greater number of people from time to time as population en-creases.

Third, When Congress shall lay direct taxes or excises, they shall immediately inform the Executive power of each State of the quota of such state according to the Census herein directed, which is proposed to be thereby raised; And if the Legislature of any State shall pass a law which shall be effectual for raising such quota at the time required by Congress, the taxes and excises laid by Congress shall not be collected, in such State.

Fourth, That the members of the Senate and House of Representatives shall be ineligible to, and incapable of holding, any civil office under the authority of the United States, during the time for which they shall respectively be elected.

Fifth, That the Journals of the proceedings of the Senate and House of Representatives shall be published at least once in every year, except such parts thereof relating to treaties, alliances or military operations, as in their judgment require secrecy.

Sixth, That a regular statement and account of the receipts and expenditures of all public money shall be published at least once in every year.

Seventh, That no commercial treaty shall be ratified without the concurrence of two thirds of the whole number of the members of the Senate; and no Treaty ceding, contracting, restraining or suspending the territorial rights or claims of the United States, or any of them or their, or any of their rights or claims to fishing in the American seas, or navigating the American rivers shall be made but in cases of the most urgent and extreme necessity, nor shall any such treaty be ratified without the concurrence of three fourths of the whole number of the members of both houses respectively.

Eighth, That no navigation law, or law regulating Commerce shall be passed without the consent of two thirds of the Members present in both houses.

Ninth, That no standing army or regular troops shall be raised or kept up in time of peace, without the consent of two thirds of the members present in both houses.

Tenth, That no soldier shall be inlisted for any longer term than four years, except in time of war, and then for no longer term than the continuance of the war.

Eleventh, That each State respectively shall have the power to provide for organizing, arming and disciplining it's own Militia, whensoever Congress shall omit or neglect to provide for the same. That the Militia shall not be subject to Martial law, except when in actual service in time of war, invasion, or rebellion; and when not in the actual service of the United States, shall be subject only to such fines, penalties and punishments as shall be directed or inflicted by the laws of its own State.

Twelfth That the exclusive power of legislation given to Congress over the Foederal Town and its adjacent District and other places purchased or to be purchased by Congress of any of the States shall extend only to such regulations as respect the police and good government thereof.

Thirteenth, That no person shall be capable of being

President of the United States for more than eight years in any term of sixteen years.

Fourteenth That the judicial power of the United States shall be vested in one supreme Court, and in such courts of Admiralty as Congress may from time to time ordain and establish in any of the different States: The Judicial power shall extend to all cases in Law and Equity arising under treaties made, or which shall be made under the authority of the United States; to all cases affecting ambassadors other foreign ministers and consuls; to all cases of Admiralty and maritime jurisdiction; to controversies to which the United States shall be a party; to controversies between two or more States, and between parties claiming lands under the grants of different States. In all cases affecting ambassadors, other foreign ministers and Consuls, and those in which a State shall be a party, the supreme court shall have original jurisdiction; in all other cases before mentioned the supreme Court shall have appellate jurisdiction as to matters of law only: except in cases of equity, and of admiralty and maritime jurisdiction, in which the Supreme Court shall have appellate jurisdiction both as to law and fact, with such exceptions and under such regulations as the Congress shall make. But the judicial power of the United States shall extend to no case where the cause of action shall have originated before the ratification of this Constitution; except in disputes between States about their Territory, disputes between persons claiming lands under the grants of different States, and suits for debts due to the United States.

Fifteenth, That in criminal prosecutions no man shall be restrained in the exercise of the usual and accustomed right of challenging or excepting to the Jury.

Sixteenth, That Congress shall not alter, modify or interfere in the times, places, or manner of holding elections for Senators and Representatives or either of them, except when the legislature of any State shall neglect, refuse or be disabled by invasion or rebellion to prescribe the same.

Seventeenth, That those clauses which declare that Congress shall not exercise certain powers be not interpreted in any manner whatsoever to extend the powers of Congress. But that they may be construed either as making exceptions to the specified powers where this shall be the case, or otherwise as inserted merely for greater caution.

Eighteenth, That the laws ascertaining the compensation to Senators and Representatives for their services be postponed in their operation, until after the election of Representatives immediately succeeding the passing thereof; that excepted, which shall first be passed on the Subject.

Nineteenth, That some Tribunal other than the Senate be provided for trying impeachments of Senators.

Twentieth, That the Salary of a Judge shall not be encreased [sic] or diminished during his continuance in Office, otherwise than by general regulations of Salary which may take place on a revision of the subject at stated periods of not less than seven years to commence from the time such Salaries shall be first ascertained by Congress.

Now let's go through the first ten Amendments as they were ratified into the Bill of Rights we now know.

The First Amendment:

"Congress shall make no law respecting an establishment of religion, or prohibiting the free exercise thereof; or abridging the freedom of speech, or of the press; or the right of the people peaceably to assemble, and to petition the Government for a redress of grievances."

The Right of Free Speech and Religion is a classic example

of Rights that have been lost by added rules and laws governing those Rights. We no longer have the 1st Amendment as it was intended. Now you must follow certain rules and laws governing religion and speech or you can be arrested, fined and or imprisoned. A classic example was the arrest of two men who started to read the bible out loud in the parking lot of a DMV office in California several years ago. There was also the arrest and conviction a couple years ago of two brothers, I briefly spoke about earlier in the book, Benjamin and Russell Bartholomew of Wheatland, Calif. who were protesting taxes in Yuba County, Calif. The Yuba County Sheriff and CHP saw a chance to get around their Constitutional right to protest by charging the two for wearing masks. The brothers had on masks as a form of political theater. It was the same mask that had become a symbol of revolt popularized in the movie V for Vendetta. The law states anyone who wears a mask while committing a crime is a violation; but these two were not committing a crime, they were Protesting Taxes. This was just another tactic the Gestapo could use to detain them. The District Attorney knew this would not stand up in court, so after a lot of research, the charge was changed to detaining an Officer from performing their duties, PC148, which was also totally bogus. The two brothers had videoed the whole incident with the sheriffs and

CHP live via direct upload to their You Tube site; http://www.youtube.com/watch?v=sG0rAkTJDmQ&feature= c4-overview-vl&list=PLE2114D1A87F51B0F for as long as it is up anyway.

The irony in all of this was a Yuba County Jury convicted the two brothers of basically Protesting Taxes, along with the crime Yuba County fabricated, which gave them a reason to arrest and charge the two. In the court trial one of the officers involved even stated under oath that he was wrong in arresting them for the charge, and yet the brainwashed jury still convicted these two brothers.

Sadly most jurors have no idea what jury nullification is; *(A Jury Voting Not Guilty if they don't agree with a crime against the defendant).* Most jurors have no idea what abuse some Judges commit against a defendant and they really don't care. There are People that don't even know that a judge can be recalled by the citizens if they feel he or she isn't following the oath that the judge swore when they were elected. When they are sworn in, they promise to uphold the Constitution of the USA and the State they are in.

Shortly after the two Brothers were sentenced and fined they went back to the same place and performed the same

Protest with an even larger Taxes=Theft sign. Only this time there were many more people with them and several Medias from newspapers to TV stations... and you know what? The local Law Enforcers did nothing this time!

This goes to show there is power in numbers and our laws in America are arbitrarily enforced or fabricated to suit the government. Unfortunately the brothers didn't appeal their conviction to a higher court because of unknown reasons. They were even told there were attorneys standing by pro-bono (No Charge) if they wanted to fight it. Well whatever the reason they still made an impact, because this is now a California precedent that can be quoted in other Protest cases.

Both Religion and Tax Protest cases clearly are a Right under the First Amendment, but the government sidestepped the Constitution by sighting other California Laws to charge the people with. Clearly doing an end run around the people's Rights, by alleging the California Laws supersede the Constitution and therefore canceling out the people's Constitutional Rights. Yet government attorneys and judges will argue these cases have nothing to do with Constitutional Rights and claim they are legally justified to charge people and convict them. Sadly the majority of the sheeple believe these outrageous lies, and those people that don't believe will rarely speak out against this tyranny.

If an individual that reads the Bible out loud and/or Protest taxes are not utilizing their Constitutional Right according to California Law Enforcers; then can be little doubt that this is a classic example of taking our First Amendment Right and turning it into a Privilege complete with rules and secondary laws to back up those rules. Thus making the First Amendment void in California or at best arbitrarily allowed. This isn't a California issue alone by any means, it happens all across the Country. But California by far is one of the worst states destroying our Constitutional Rights in the Nation. Followed closely by New York, two of the most populated states, which set the stage for the federal government changing the meaning of your Rights.

Many of our States deliberately refuse to allow people to enjoy their Constitutional Rights, especially when the government in control disapproves of a Right Granted in the Bill of Rights such as the Second Amendment.

Second Amendment in the Bill of Rights:

You can judge for yourselves what our Founding Fathers had in mind when they wrote the Second Amendment.

As passed by Congress and preserved in the National Archives: *"A well regulated Militia, being necessary to the security of a free State, the right of the people to keep and bear Arms, shall not be infringed."*

This once guaranteed Right has now also been labeled a Privilege complete with laws and rules that totally go against the Second Amendment. Thirty years ago you could buy a handgun or rifle from most anyone, anywhere in California. You could even walk down the end of a street into the fields, forest, deserts and wild lands with your gun to go hunting or target practice without anyone going through convulsions over it. Then the Progressives and Socialists got control and spat on the Constitution and started the Infringement of the Second Amendment.

The Second Amendment clearly states that the "RIGHT" to bear arms "SHALL NOT BE INFRINGED" yet in California they recently passed a no open carry law against all Guns. This means if you openly carry a gun in public and show it, use it, sell it, or do not register or buy it through a STATE LICENSED DEALER; It can and will be used against you in a court of law that will make you out to look like a criminal, and then they will take away your RIGHT TO BEAR ARMS! We have lost that right! Because the once freer people of this once freer country were complacently apathetic and allowed that freedom to be taken from them.

The politicians and law enforcers who work fervently to try and convince the people that this is not INFRINGING on their Rights, honestly believe that The People are that stupid and will fall for it. Unfortunately they have been proven right, because the people really have done nothing to stop this Unconstitutional downright outward tyrannical theft and abuse of our second amendment Right.

Elected officials like Dianne Feinstein a US Senator from California, and State Senator Darrel Steinberg, really seem to hate the Constitution. They especially hate the Second Amendment. Feinstein and Steinberg have repeatedly tried to destroy the Second Amendment and Feinstein stated in a media interview; *"If I could have gotten 51 votes in the Senate I would have said Mr. and Mrs. America turn in your guns."* - Dianne Feinstein told the interviewer this after her failed attempts to repeal the Second Amendment. They now are going after ammunition, and have passed a law banning lead bullets in California. How in the mind of any sane person is that not infringing on our Right to Bear Arms?

People in the government like Feinstein, Steinberg, Boxer, Pelosi and Obama, and those in the socialist media like British commentator Piers Morgan work tirelessly to destroy the Constitution by using fear and bogus statistics to sway public opinion and to disarm Americans and further enslave them. The Second Amendment was put in place to protect us from the Government... And that is a fact that your master government doesn't like, and is going to put an end to unless you rise up against that tyranny!

The government has successfully gained control of the handguns with their laws that circumvent the Second Amendment. These laws make it too expensive and/or too regulated for most citizens to afford or be approved to legally bear those arms. So that is an infringement, and even being forced to register a gun is an infringement.

The US Government has totally ignored the Constitution when it comes to our Second Amendment Right. States like California, New York, Illinois and the District of Columbia are totally against the Second Amendment and have violated the people's Right to Bear Arms. Because of the Second Amendment Violations, Chicago and DC, which have the strictest gun laws in the nation, also have the highest Gun Related Murder rates in the country. The Federal Government and Supreme Court has also allowed States like California and New York to violate the Second Amendment, as well as all of our Rights in the Constitution with contempt. Many will argue that the Second Amendment is mostly still intact, but it is not!

The 1968 Federal Gun Control Act shown below proves how the Second Amendment has been whittled down over the years:

"Under the United States Gun Control Act of 1968, any cartridge firearm made in or before 1898 ("pre-1899") is classified as an "antique", and is generally outside of Federal jurisdiction, as administered and enforced by the U.S. Bureau of Alcohol, Tobacco, Firearms and Explosives (BATFE). The only exceptions to the Federal exemption are antique machineguns (such as the Maxim gun and Colt Model 1895 potato digger) and antique cartridge rifles or shotguns firing shotgun shells that are classified as "short barreled" per the U.S. Gun Control Act of 1968, namely cartridge rifles with a barrel less than 16 inches long, or shotguns firing shotgun shells with a barrel less than 18 inches long, or either cartridge rifles or shotgun-shell-

firing shotguns with an overall length of less than 26 inches. Muzzleloading guns, as replicas of antique guns, are not subject to Federal jurisdiction and are essentially classified the same as an antique gun. Hence, a muzzleloading black-powder shotgun is not subject to the short-barreled National Firearms Act of 1934 restrictions. Purchases of such modern-day manufactured replicas may be done outside of the normal Federal Firearms License (FFL) restrictions that otherwise exist when purchasing modern (post-1898) guns. Replicas of cartridge-firing rifles, however, are not classed the same as antiques, but must be purchased through FFL holders, although a true antique that was manufactured prior to 1899 firing the same cartridge as the replica would be legal for sale without the transfer being processed through an FFL. Furthermore, any rifle re-built on a receiver or frame that was manufactured prior to 1899 is considered antique, even if it has been re-barreled or even if every other part has been replaced.

The following is an excerpt from the portion of the Gun Control Act of 1968 (which modified Title 18, U.S. Code) that exempted pre-1899 guns from the Federal Firearms

License paperwork requirements administered by the BATFE:

18 USC 921 (a)(16). (A) any firearm (including any firearm with a matchlock, flintlock, percussion cap, or similar type of ignition system) manufactured in or before 1898; and (B) any replica of any firearm described in subparagraph (A) if such replica -- (i) is not designed or redesigned for using rimfire or conventional centerfire fixed ammunition, or (ii) uses rimfire or conventional centerfire fixed ammunition which is no longer manufactured in the United States and which is not readily available in the ordinary channels of commercial trade.

Within the United States, antique exemptions vary considerably from state to state.

Identifying pre-1899 antiques

The production of many cartridge firearms, such as the famous Winchester Model 1894 lever action rifle took place both before and after the December 31, 1898 cut-off date that delineates exempt antique status under U.S. law. Therefore, collectors rely on references such as The Pre-1899 Antique Guns FAQ by James Wesley Rawles to determine if a particular gun's serial number falls within the range of "antique" (pre-1899) production. For example, a Winchester Model 1894 with serial number 147,685 had its frame (or "receiver") made in December 1898 and it is hence classified as an "antique", but records show that a Winchester Model 1894 with serial number 147,686 had its frame made in January, 1899 and it is hence classified as "modern" by the BATFE therefore, black powder weapons are not firearms unless said black powder weapon can be converted to propel rim-fire ammunition.

Since it is the date of manufacture of the receiver that is relevant to identifying a gun as antique or modern, it is possible to have a weapon with date marks post-1898 but still be considered an antique gun. For example, some Finnish M39 (Ukko-Pekka) Mosin-Nagant rifles with hexagonal profile receivers are considered antique because some were built on receivers dated pre-1899, even though the rifle itself was adopted in 1939. Many of these were assembled using a mix of old round and "hex" receivers from then on, until as late as the 1970s. To be identified as pre-1899, however, Mosin-Nagants that have been re-barreled must be disassembled to see the date stamps on their tangs. A similar situation exists for 7.65mm Mauser

Turkish Model 1893 bolt actions, most of which were re-arsenalized at the Ankara arsenal in the 1940s, and re-chambered to 8x57mm Mauser. Despite this re-arsenalization and re-chambering, they are still considered antiques under US law as all rifles of that model were manufactured between 1893 and 1896. Likewise, all firearms produced by Ludwig Loewe & Co. A.G., which are marked "Ludwig Loewe" or "Loewe, Berlin", are antiques. This is because Ludwig Loewe was merged into Deutsche Waffen und Munitionsfabriken in 1897, and the Loewe name was no longer used after the merger.

In the case United States vs. Kirvan, He was charged with Armed Robbery and a Felon in possession of a firearm while committing a felony. Kirvan was found guilty of the armed robbery but was found innocent of being a felon in possession of a firearm while committing a felony charge; due to the fact that a black powder weapon is not considered a firearm under the definition of federal gun laws. It was added that a black powder weapon that has never been used or shot before, classifies it as a display piece which does not consider it a firearm. Therefore the judge had to dismiss the charge.

So now only Black Powder guns are legal under the Second Amendment in the Constitution according to the Federal

Government. But in Washington DC a man was arrested and convicted for having a Lead Ball bullet from a Black Powder gun in 2014. These treasonous traitors against the Second Amendment have assumed criminalizing ammo will be just as effective as an all out ban on guns. These treasonous traitors have been totally against what the Second Amendment stands for and have been trying to change the meaning of the 2nd Amendment for well over 130 years. After all their propaganda and down right lies, with little resistance from the general masses, they have successfully managed to change our Second Amendment and believe me they are not going to stop there!

In United States v. Cruikshank, 92 U.S. 542 (1875), the Supreme Court ruled that; *"The right to bear arms is not granted by the Constitution; neither is it in any manner dependent upon that instrument for its existence. The Second Amendment means no more than that it shall not be infringed by Congress, and has no other effect than to restrict the powers of the 'National Government.'"* This was shortly after the Civil War and the government was eager to limit the people's ability to wage war against the government ever again. So they gave power to the States to ban guns Un-Constitutionally, which was later over ruled in a Supreme

Court ruling that stated to ban guns would violate a persons Second Amendment. So now the governments both State and Federal impose laws making it almost impossible to own a gun, or use it, without extensive paperwork and major expense due to the high taxes and fees gun manufacturers have to pay which is passes on you the gun buyer.

Other Supreme Court Cases that further confused the Second Amendment Right are: In the *District of Columbia v. Heller*, 554 U.S. 570 (2008**), the Supreme Court ruled that the Second Amendment *"Codified a pre-existing Right"* and that it protects an individuals Right to possess a firearm unconnected with service in a militia, and to use that arm for traditional lawful purpose, such as self-defense within the home. It also stated; *"that the right is not unlimited. It is not a right to keep and carry any weapon whatsoever in any manner whatsoever and for whatever purpose"*. They also clarified that many longstanding prohibitions and restrictions on firearm possession listed by the Court are consistent with the Second Amendment. Which was just a manipulation of the Constitution and Second Amendment to control the Right to own a gun!

In *McDonald v. Chicago*, 561 U.S. 3025 (2010), the Supreme Court ruled that the Second Amendment limits state and local government to the same extent that it limits the federal government.

This hasn't stopped the States and Federal government from issuing laws and rules attached to our Constitutional Right under the Second Amendment. The government both federal and state, have for the most part ignored High Court rulings because they know it takes a lot of resource and a long time for anyone or any group to get a challenge to the Supreme Court, and by the time they do, most people will have become complacent and excepted whatever illegal unconstitutional law that has been imposed and enforced on them. Only the Government (Federal & State) or large corporations with the financial resource are able to fight in the High Court arena, unless public outcry is widespread, and then the High Court may rule on the issue.

Our Government seems to be able to change so many of our rights at the drop of a dime. If it can help them win a case or they just want to show their power and show us they are our masters, they will do whatever is necessary to win! Since we are being hijacked by Social Leftist and fascits who pretend they are Constitutionalist, and fool Presidents into appointing them to the Supreme Court. We The Citizens of America need to be able to Amend our Constitution to allow

The Supreme Court Justice to be overruled if three fourths of the State disagree with their ruling. Then it should go to a vote of the people to either invalidate or ratify. This would give back the state their right that was granted them under the 10th Amendment of the Constitution; especially since we have seen totally Unconstitutional Laws/Taxes passed by the Supreme Court over the years. The Supreme Court Justice should also have a term limit just as the President does, the reasoning behind this is pretty obvious. When an official is elected and they turn out to be bad and pass unconstitutional laws and regulations, we vote then out. So we need to be able to get Supreme Court Justices out or have some solace in knowing that their time is limited. The President is only elected for a 4 year term and can do a lot of damage in that time, but we can choose to not elect them again in the next term. A Supreme Court Justice is in there for life and can really make some bad judgements that could shatter our Constitutional Rights, and when they do there is no way to get them out, or change their ruling!

This was the ratified wording from the States and authenticated by Thomas Jefferson, then Secretary of State:

"A well regulated militia being necessary to the security of a free state, the right of the people to keep and bear arms shall

not be infringed."

Free people should not have to ask for permission in a free Country... especially when it comes down to your Guaranteed Amendment Rights! This is something you might think about if you ever have to ask permission from your government to use a Guaranteed Freedom that was clearly defined in the Bill of Rights as part of the Constitution. If any of your government officials laugh at you when you mention your rights, ask them if they swore an oath to uphold the Constitution? If they did, then why are they laughing, because the loss of freedom is no laughing matter, is it?

The Picture Below Is Now Happening In America!

Chinese police drown confiscated firearms in gasoline before setting them on fire. The Chinese Government routinely destroys civilian firearms in an effort to maintain absolute power.

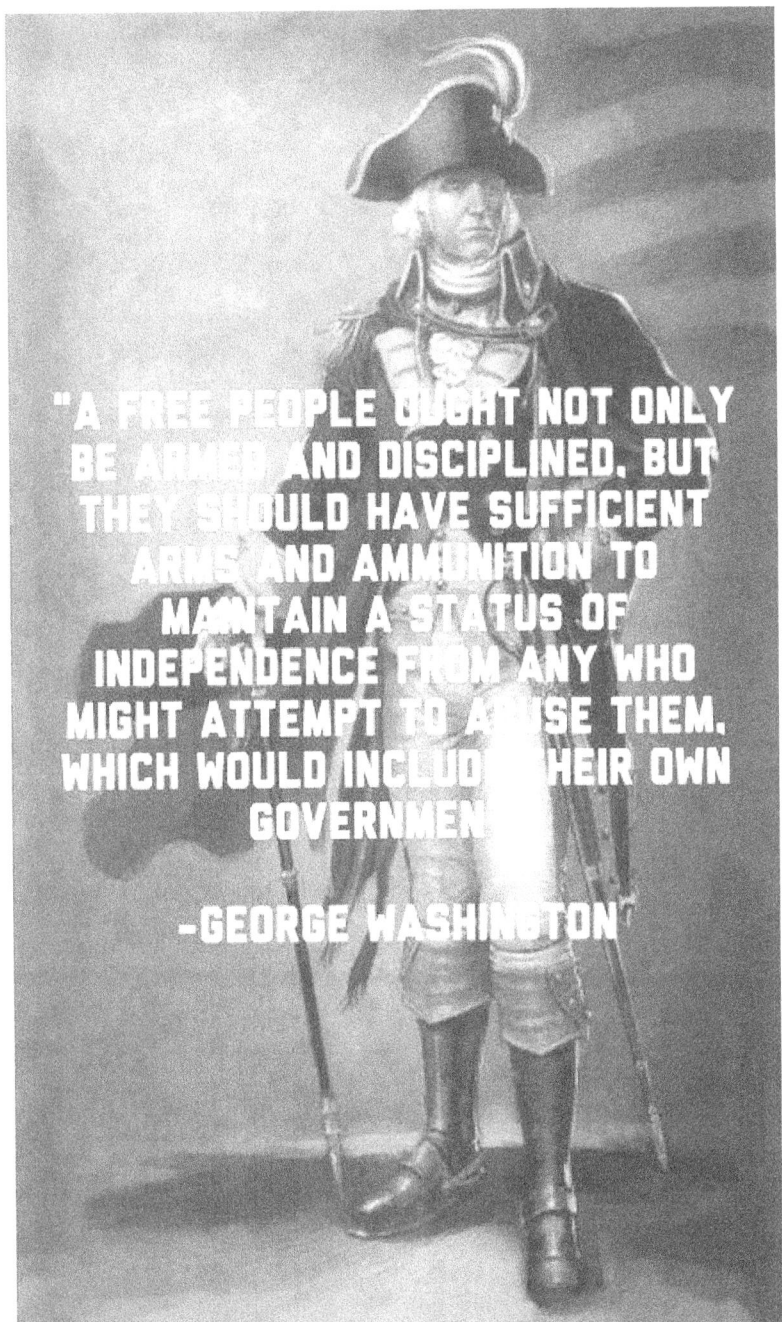

The Third Amendment:

"No Soldier shall, in time of peace be quartered in any house, without the consent of the Owner, nor in time of war, but in a manner to be prescribed by law."

The Third Amendment to the United States Constitution places restrictions on the quartering of soldiers in private homes without the owner's consent, forbidding the practice in peacetime. The amendment is a response to Quartering Acts passed by the British parliament during the American Revolutionary War that allowed the British Army to lodge soldiers in private residences. Basically they would take a persons home and use it for as long as it was in their interest and loot it and many times burn it to the ground.

But today the government can easily get around the Third Amendment by declaring marshal law against an unknown terrorist, which they claim they are at war with. Or telling the citizens there is a national security threat that they can't tell you about as they point their M16s and AR15s at you as they escort you out of your home and off of your property.

Fourth Amendment:

"The right of the people to be secure in their persons, houses, papers, and effects, against unreasonable searches and seizures, shall not be violated, and no Warrants shall issue, but upon probable cause, supported by Oath or affirmation, and particularly describing the place to be searched, and the persons or things to be seized."

The Fourth Amendment governing search and seizure has been shredded and is basically just words with no meaning as far as the government is concerned. It is supposed to prohibit unreasonable search and seizure and requires a warrant to be judicially sanctioned by a Judge and supported by probable cause. It was adopted in response to the abuse of the writ of assistance, a type of general search warrant issued by the British Government and a major source of tension in pre-Revolutionary America. The government of today has reintroduced the Writ of Assistance by allowing a Judge to sign a blank warrant that law enforcers can use without contacting a judge. These warrants are a Blanket Warrant that covers everything and anything, basically allowing police to kick in your door when ever they want. Or search anyone when ever they want even a baby in a wheelchair! This is happening across the nation right now and no one is standing up to this tyranny…

The Picture on the next page was taken by little 3 year old Lucy's Parents at an airport, shows little Lucy in a wheelchair being terrorized by Gestapo thug TSA. This poor little girl was supposed to be on a vacation of her little life to Disney World, instead the bastards at the airport turned this little happy crippled girl's dream adventure into a nightmare that will scare her forever!

When I saw this cell phone video, I couldn't help but get emotional over this poor crippled terrorized little 3-year old. This could have been one of my own grand children, and I had nothing but violent hate for those who did this! I still think those TSA should be tracked down and made to pay for their terrorist actions against a child! This was no doubt child abuse at its worse because your own government sanctioned it, which is above all laws that you have to obey!

As a parent or grand parent you can never allow a ruthless government Gestapo thug to get away with assaulting your kid(s) without retaliation. They have to be hunted down and brought to justice because what they have done is commit a wantin' act of war against you and your family!

Look as the terror on that little girls face...if that doesn't bring a tear to your eye, you are already enslaved!

Lucy: "I don't wanna go to Disney World!"

The 4th Amendment is a very important Right that is ignored by most of the States and the Federal Government, and I think the 4th Amendment has been abused the most by our government.

Sadly it is each and every one of our faults, because we have done nothing to stop the abuse. We allow these liars and power hungry manipulators to stay in power; even after they have proven they have no intention of representing the people that they were elected to represent or protect the Constitution. We have to stop thinking they will change and we have to stop voting for them or we are surely doomed to slavery.

I can also point out the NSA spying on all Americans without a warrant. Edward Snowden totally overturned the applecart and opened up a big can of worms for the government with that little revelation. Unfortunately, little to nothing will ever be done by our government to stop this. So we have no 4th Amendment anymore.

This poor family (next page) was ordered out of their home at gunpoint in Boston... No Warrant just kick in the doors and order the residents out. If they refuse they can be shot and killed and no court in the country will prosecute the Gestapo, because they believe the government's authority overrides the citizens Rights when they deem there is a threat to the Government! If this isn't a violation of the 4th Amendment, I don't know what is?

Another fallacy is that you don't have to show ID if asked by police/Gestapo and this is a cloudy issue that the Supreme Court has basically ruled on that says you DO have to show your papers in most cases.

Do you have to show an ID if asked by Police/Gestapo? Well in Hiibel v. Sixth Judicial District Court of Nevada, the U.S. Supreme Court upheld the conviction of Larry Dudley Hiibel, who was standing next to his pick-up truck on the passenger's side when a sheriff drove by and asked him if he knew anything about a fight in the area. Mr. Hiibel said he knew nothing about a fight. Then the sheriff asked him for ID and he refused since he was doing nothing wrong. Well he was arrested and convicted of a misdemeanor and fined 250 dollars. Since the Supreme Court upheld his conviction, it requires that persons stopped under Terry rules, MUST show ID, but persons not suspected of a crime do not.

Of course the police/Gestapo now routinely lie and tell people they had a report of some bogus crime in the area which then forces you to have to show ID or you can face arrest. Just one more example of government shredding our Rights, and taking away our freedom. So we have no choice but to obey and worship the very thing the Constitution was written to control, the government, and the very thing our founding fathers fought and died for... Freedom from Government Oppression!

The Fifth Amendment:

"No person shall be held to answer for a capital, or otherwise infamous crime, unless on a presentment or indictment of a Grand Jury, except in cases arising in the land or naval forces, or in the Militia, when in actual

service in time of War or public danger; nor shall any person be subject for the same offence to be twice put in jeopardy of life or limb; nor shall be compelled in any criminal case to be a witness against himself, nor be deprived of life, liberty, or property, without due process of law; nor shall private property be taken for public use, without just compensation. "

The Fifth Amendment has been ignored and has been deemed as Not a Defense in court after court. Unless you are the head of the IRS or some other elite head of a government agency. This Amendment is extremely important to Freedom and people have stood aside and said nothing, allowing it to become null and void. I have seen people attempt to use their 4th and 5th Amendment Rights when being abused by Law Enforcers. These law enforcers who swore an oath to uphold the Constitution and Bill of Rights, just laugh between each other and say, Ha, he thinks he knows his Rights, we'll show him how much he knows." Then they arrest that person without just cause. The Gestapo calls this a P.O.P. charge as I stated earlier, which if you forgot means (Pissing Off Police).

Judges have totally thrown out the 5th Amendment defense in most cases and force people to talk by intimidation of contempt, jail time and fines. I have heard judges tell defendants who try and use the 5th Amendment that it doesn't apply in their case and they had to talk or they would be jailed for contempt of court. On the other hand I have also heard defense attorneys say that they have to see the same Judges in their courtroom day after day, so they have to watch what they say, even if the Judge is totally wrong and the defendant has the 5th Amendment Right on their side. The attorney does not want to piss off the judge by objecting.

I have come to the realization that if you want an attorney who will not be scared of pissing off the judge, you have to go outside your local area to find one. And it is going to cost you, but it is worth it if you want to win against a system that only cares about numbers convicted, not if you are innocent.

The Sixth Amendment:

"In all criminal prosecutions, the accused shall enjoy the right to a speedy and public trial, by an impartial jury of the State and district wherein the crime shall have been committed, which district shall have been previously ascertained by law, and to be informed of the nature and cause of the accusation; to be confronted with the witnesses against him; to have compulsory process for obtaining

witnesses in his favor, and to have the Assistance of Counsel for his defense."

I don't think you have to look too far to see this Amendment has also been shredded and twisted to serve the courts and not those accused of a crime. Since the advent of the cell phone and video cameras, more and more people are video taping crimes by both citizen and law enforcers, and time and time again police seize the recording device and erase or destroy them which is directly in violation of the 1st, 4th and 5th Amendments.

The Courts are also routinely refusing to allow many of these recorded violations to be seen, especially if it shows law enforcers are the ones breaking the law with civil Rights violations. The reason for this is the courts have given police/Gestapo supreme powers and they are above the laws you and I have to follow. The Judges know many of these recorded videos of police abusing their authority would indeed sway a jury to nullify charges against a defendant. So they block the jury from viewing them.

The Police/Gestapo can lie to you and the court and nothing can be done about it, because they have been given immunity by the government and we have allowed this abuse of power to grow.

If a crime is capped with a 6 month prison sentence YOU HAVE NO 6th AMENDMENT RIGHT to a jury trial if you are arrested for acts of civil disobedience, according to U.S. District Judge Dale A. Drozd of California who has sited a Supreme Court Ruling which basically destroyed the 6th Amendment. In other words, if you are arrested for protesting without permission to do so, you automatically are looking at 6 months in prison.

So much for the 6th Amendment of the Bill of Rights…it is gone! It's like a judge slapping contempt of court/government charge on you and locking you up for 6 months for protesting or basically any crime with a max 6 months in jail. Because of this the 1st Amendment has become worthless as well.

The Seventh Amendment:

"In Suits at common law, where the value in controversy shall exceed twenty dollars, the right of trial by jury shall be preserved, and no fact tried by a jury, shall be otherwise re-examined in any Court of the United States, than according to the rules of the common law."

Once again the 7th Amendment is also ignored. Anytime you see "mandatory arbitration" in any warrantee on any item you buy, or when signing up for telephone service, cable, gas and electric, or even signing to be seen by a doctor, or buying a new car, you are signing away your 7th Amendment Right, and the odds are stacked against you. Most times you have no recourse to appeal a decision and it's stated that all decisions are final.

The right to file a civil complaint in federal court has been shredded by the Supreme Court's decision on *Iqbal* and the *Twombly* cases. I have to wonder if this wasn't deliberate since it created new harder standards for filing a civil suit against a corporation, and it will no doubt get worse with the new interpretations/rewriting of the 7th Amendment each time one of the appeal courts get to it. The 7th shredding started in 1950 with a Supreme Court decision that pretty much gives governments and government contractor's exemption from being sued for negligence.

Trying to recover from negligence at the hands of the government or military or a government contractor with billions of dollars in government contracts, probably isn't going to happen no matter how blatant the negligence was. So the Corporate Government has made sure it's protected from the people by changing the rules contrary to what the 7th Amendment of the Constitution clearly states... And once again the people are guilty of complacently apathetic about all this manipulation of the Bill of Rights. Unfortunately many of the people are also ignorant and have never learned about the Constitution and Bill of Rights in public schools. Or have learned only what the school wanted them to learn and that has been proven to be selective teaching by omission.

The Eighth Amendment:

"Excessive bail shall not be required, nor excessive fines imposed, nor cruel and unusual punishments inflicted."

This Amendment is gone altogether since President Obama signed into law a bill that lets the government imprison American Citizens deemed to be a possible combatant without Bail or Trial forever if they want. On December 31, 2011, President Barack Obama signed the National Defense Authorization Act, NDAA, that was ratified in 2013 when it passed the Senate with a 98-0 vote. The authorization gave the government the ability to be able to detain American Citizens without a trial indefinitely, eliminating habeas corpus for the American people.

The Ninth Amendment:

"The enumeration in the Constitution, of certain rights, shall not be construed to deny or disparage others retained by the people."

The Ninth Amendment was supposed to give inalienable Rights you never knew you had. But it too has been ignored by the government, and since few people know about the Ninth Amendment, which reaffirms in pretty broad terms the rights "retained by the people"; Those in power have pretend that it really doesn't exist.

The right to die, or what you can do to, or with, your own body, and the right to do whatever you want with your own property were "Unremunerated" Rights including, the right to privacy The Founding Fathers were trying to acknowledge some of the rights that no government could deny free people. But of course that didn't stop the government from denying those freedoms to all the people.

Now all you do, own, say, and think are controlled so the Ninth Amendment has become void in the eyes of the government.

The Tenth Amendment:

"The powers not delegated to the United States by the Constitution, nor prohibited by it to the States, are reserved to the States respectively, or to the people."

Well of course this is another Right ignored and abused. Wikipedia sums it up: "The Tenth Amendment is similar to an earlier provision of the Articles of Confederation: "Each state retains its sovereignty, freedom, and independence, and every power, jurisdiction, and right, which is not by this Confederation expressly delegated to the United States, in Congress assembled." After the Constitution was ratified, some wanted to add a similar amendment limiting the federal government to powers "expressly" delegated, which would have denied implied powers. However, the word "expressly" ultimately did not appear in the Tenth Amendment as ratified, and therefore the Tenth Amendment did not reject the powers implied by the Necessary and Proper Clause."

When James Madison introduced the Tenth Amendment in Congress, he explained that many states were eager to ratify this amendment, despite critics who deemed the amendment superfluous or unnecessary: *"I find, from looking into the amendments proposed by the State conventions, that several are particularly anxious that it should be declared in the Constitution, that the powers not therein delegated should be reserved to the several States. Perhaps words which may define this more precisely than the whole of the instrument now does, may be considered as superfluous. I admit they may be deemed unnecessary: but there can be no harm in making such a declaration, if gentlemen will allow that the fact is as stated. I am sure I understand it so, and do therefore propose it"- James Madison.*

The Constitution and the Bill of Rights are gone as far as the government is concerned... unless they need to use it for themselves. Consequently because we have allowed this to happen, American Justice has become a joke monarchy or a dictatorship and it is persecution and prosecution by discretion. There is nothing fair or impartial about it... it is all about whom you know and who you are, and as long as you have some public support and a lot of political support, your chances of being charged or convicted of a crime are slim. If you don't have a lot of support, or know someone in a high place and you get arrested for even the smallest offence, with the most flimsy of circumstantial evidence, or even if you are totally innocent and get arrested on some totally bogus charge. You are either going to have to pony up a large sum of money to an attorney, thousands, tens of thousands or hundreds of thousands, and prey you get off, or you will be spending money on fines and maybe even time with big Elmo or Elma in a prison cell.

****

"Truth is stranger than fiction, but it is because Fiction is obliged to stick to possibilities; Truth isn't." — Mark Twain.

Here are a few movies to watch and books to read. Some tried to warn future populations of rising threats, and some seem to have eerily predicted the future.

1984 by George Orwell 1984.

In a totalitarian future society, a man, whose daily work is re-writing history, tries to rebel by falling in love, which is forbidden by the State.

Animal Farm by George Orwell 1954.

This film is a cartoon adaptation of George Orwell's parable expressing the founding of

the USSR and the reign of Stalin.
The animals are tired of being under the cruel
hand of Farmer Jones (Czar Nicholas II), so
Old Major (Karl Marx), a pig, leads a meeting
declaring that man is their enemy.

Flu 2013. (English Sub Titled)

Chaos ensues when a lethal, airborne virus
H5N1 Corona Virus is introduced and infects
the population of a South Korean city less
than 20 kilometers from Seoul, all infected die
within 36 hours.

CELL a book by Stephen King 2006

When a mysterious cell phone signal causes
apocalyptic chaos, an artist is determined to
reunite with his young son in New England.

Utopia, 2013 Rated M

Utopia is a British series that is a kind of Alice in
Wonderland on LSD science fiction thriller. This
flick has some real eerie futuristic possibilities
about planned overt pandemics in the future.

Chapter V

Destroying the Constitution with Healthcare and the Takeover of Medicine

Socialist Affordable Healthcare, which is un-constitutionally imposed no matter what the Supreme Court tells the public, is the biggest lie the American people ever had to swallow. It really has nothing to do with making people healthy; it has to do with totally destroying the Constitution and Seizing total control over the American People's Bodies.

I know the medical industry has its problems and has had problems for a long time. I know from first hand experience that it has gotten as corrupt as the government because of the government involvement. I also know that the medical industry is as full of liars as our government. I refuse to go to any doctor that lies to me and I have caught several liars. My philosophy is real simple; If a Doctor, namely Your Doctor lies to you about any of your medical care, how the hell can you trust them with your health? When I catch a healthcare individual boldfaced lying to me, I will call them on that lie, and if they persist, I normally just put on my hat and walk out. Unless I am in an exceptionally aggravated state, then I will put on my hat and tell them they are fired, and then walk out never to return.

Years ago when I was a kid you could call a doctor and they would make a house call. Now you can't get a doctor to return your phone call. Years ago the doctor or nurse or their staff never lied to you by telling you that because you take this or that medication you have to come in every 30 days, and I am not talking about class 2 drugs. Now doctors and staff routinely lie out their pie-holes to people and I have caught them at it. It is all revenue generation, and if lying gets the job done, then they are going to lie to you! They are now just as bad, and even worse, than the Politicians and Gestapo because your life and general health is in their hands. That is a sad epitaph for medical in the USA, and it is getting harder and harder to find a good old country doctor. Because they are being replaced with government taught brown-nose medical lackeys that could care less about your health only about the bottom financial line and pleasing big pharma and their government masters.

I am often asked; "Well what can you do?" and the answer is simple, don't do business with manipulating liars! Shun them and tell people who they are and refuse to accept the excuses they use to explain their lies! Especially, if you catch them in a boldfaced lie that was aimed at you to control you!

Now on with Health laws, which was sold to the American people by lies, and now to be enforced by the Government, which is run by Bold Faced Liars, you can pretty much expect to be lied to about the real agenda of the government. And that is total control over you their slave property! You Better Obey when they tell you to get an injection or Obey their medical edicts.

This is a letter from a former Constitutional Lawyer that was posted on the Internet that tells the real truth:

"The Truth About the Health Care Act" - Michael Connelly, Ret. Constitutional Attorney

"Well, I have done it! I have read the entire text of proposed House Bill 3200: The Affordable Health Care Choices Act of 2009. I studied it with particular emphasis from my area of expertise, constitutional law. I was frankly concerned that parts of the proposed law that were being discussed might be unconstitutional.

What I found was far worse than what I had heard or expected.

To begin with, much of what has been said about the law

and its implications is in fact true, despite what the Democrats and the media are saying. The law does provide for rationing of health care, particularly where senior citizens and other classes of citizens are involved, free health care for illegal immigrants, free abortion services, and probably forced participation in abortions by members of the medical profession.

The Bill will also eventually force private insurance companies out of business, and put everyone into a government run system. All decisions about personal health care will ultimately be made by federal bureaucrats, and most of them will not be health care professionals. The government will strictly control hospital admissions, payments to physicians, and allocations of necessary medical devices.

However, as scary as all of that is, it just scratches the surface. In fact, I have concluded that this legislation really has no intention of providing affordable health care choices. Instead it is a convenient cover for the most massive transfer of power to the Executive Branch of government that has ever occurred, or even been contemplated. If this law or a similar one is adopted, major portions of the Constitution of the United States will effectively have been destroyed.

The first thing to go will be the masterfully crafted balance of power between the Executive, Legislative, and Judicial branches of the U.S. Government. The Congress will be transferring to the Obama Administration authority in a number of different areas over the lives of the American people, and the businesses they own.

The irony is that the Congress doesn't have any authority to legislate in most of those areas to begin with! I defy anyone to read the text of the U.S. Constitution and find any authority granted to the members of Congress to regulate health care.

This legislation also provides for access, by the appointees of the Obama administration, all of your personal healthcare information, a direct violation of the specific provisions of the 4th Amendment to the Constitution, information, your personal financial information, and the information of your employer, physician, and hospital. All of this is a protecting against unreasonable searches and seizures. You can also forget about the right to privacy. That will have been legislated into oblivion regardless of what the 3rd and 4th Amendments may provide.

If you decide not to have healthcare insurance, or if you have private insurance that is not deemed acceptable to the Health Choices Administrator appointed by Obama, there will be a tax imposed on you. It is called a tax instead of a fine because of the intent to avoid application of the due process clause of the 5th Amendment. However, that doesn't work because since there is nothing in the law that allows you to contest or appeal the imposition of the tax, it is definitely depriving someone of property without the due process of law.

So, there are three of those pesky Amendments that the far left hate so much, out of the original ten in the Bill of Rights, that are effectively nullified by this law. It doesn't stop there though.

The 9th Amendment that provides: The enumeration in the Constitution, of certain rights, shall not be construed to deny or disparage others retained by the people;

The 10th Amendment states: The powers not delegated to the United States by the Constitution, nor prohibited by it to the States, are preserved to the States respectively, or to the people. Under the provisions of this piece of Congressional handiwork neither the people nor the states are going to have any rights or powers at all in many areas that once were theirs to control.

I could write many more pages about this legislation, but I think you get the idea. This is not about health care; it is about seizing power and limiting rights. Article 6 of the Constitution requires the members of both houses of Congress to "be bound by oath or affirmation to support the Constitution." If I was a member of Congress I would not be able to vote for this legislation or anything like it, without feeling I was violating that sacred oath or affirmation. If I voted for it anyway, I would hope the American people would hold me accountable.

For those who might doubt the nature of this threat, I suggest they consult the source, the U.S. Constitution, and Bill of Rights. There you can see exactly what we are about to have taken from us."

Here are some points to consider that Doctor Ron Paul had writen that are right on target:

"No one has a right to medical care. If one assumes such a right, it endorses the notion that some individuals have a right to someone else's life and property. This totally contradicts the principles of liberty.

If medical care is provided by government, this can only be achieved by an authoritarian government unconcerned about the rights of the individual.

Economic fallacies accepted for more than 100 years in the United States has deceived policy makers into believing that quality medical care can only be achieved by government force, taxation, regulations, and bowing to a system of special interests that creates a system of corporatism.

More dollars into any monopoly run by government never increases quality but it always results in higher costs and prices.

Government does have an important role to play in facilitating the delivery of all goods and services in an ethical and efficient manner.

First, government should do no harm. It should get out of the way and repeal all the laws that have contributed to the mess we have.

The costs are obviously too high but in solving this problem one cannot ignore the debasement of the currency as a major factor.

Bureaucrats and other third parties must never be allowed to interfere in the doctor/patient relationship.

The tax code, including the ERISA laws, must be changed to give everyone equal treatment by allowing a 100% tax credit for all medical expenses.

Laws dealing with bad outcomes and prohibiting doctors from entering into voluntary agreements with their patients must be repealed. Tort laws play a significant role in pushing costs higher, prompting unnecessary treatment and excessive testing. Patients deserve the compensation; the attorneys do not.

Insurance sales should be legalized nationally across state lines to increase competition among the insurance companies.

Long-term insurance policies should be available to young people similar to term-life insurances that offer fixed prices for long periods of time.

The principle of insurance should be remembered. Its purpose in a free market is to measure risk, not to be used synonymously with social welfare programs. Any program that provides for first-dollar payment is no longer insurance. This would be similar to giving coverage for gasoline and repair bills to those who buy car insurance or providing food insurance for people to go to the grocery store. Obviously, that could not work. The cozy relationship between organized medicine and government must be reversed.

Early on medical insurance was promoted by the medical community in order to boost re-imbursements to doctors and hospitals. That partnership has morphed into the government/insurance industry still being promoted by the current administration.

Threatening individuals with huge fines by forcing them to buy insurance is a boon to the insurance companies. There must be more competition for individuals entering into the medical field. Licensing strictly limits the number of individuals who can provide patient care. A lot of problems were created in 20th century as a consequence the Flexner Report (1910), which was financed by the Carnegie Foundation and strongly supported by the AMA. Many medical schools were closed and the number of doctors was drastically reduced. The motivation was to close down medical schools that catered to women, minorities and especially homeopathy. We continue to suffer from these changes which were designed to protect physician's income and promote allopathic medicine over the more natural cures and prevention of homeopathic medicine.

We must remove any obstacles for people seeking holistic and nutritional alternatives to current medical care. We must remove the threat of further regulations pushed by the drug companies now working worldwide to limit these alternatives." – Doctor Ron Paul

Those who think Socialized Medicine is a good thing never considered that once the government takes total control over medicine, you lose control of your own body. They can demand you get medical procedures by claiming you pose a health threat to society. Once they fool the sheeple into believing you are a threat...the people will demand they do something about you! This healthcare nightmare and cost problem never existed before 1965 when the government signed into law Medicare and took control and dictated how and what hospitals and doctors could do. That was the moment President Johnson signed the Medicare law and costs started to skyrocket!

Below is a chart that shows the rise after 1965 that proves when government gets control you pay more! Costs have skyrocketed since the Government has gotten involve in your healthcare.

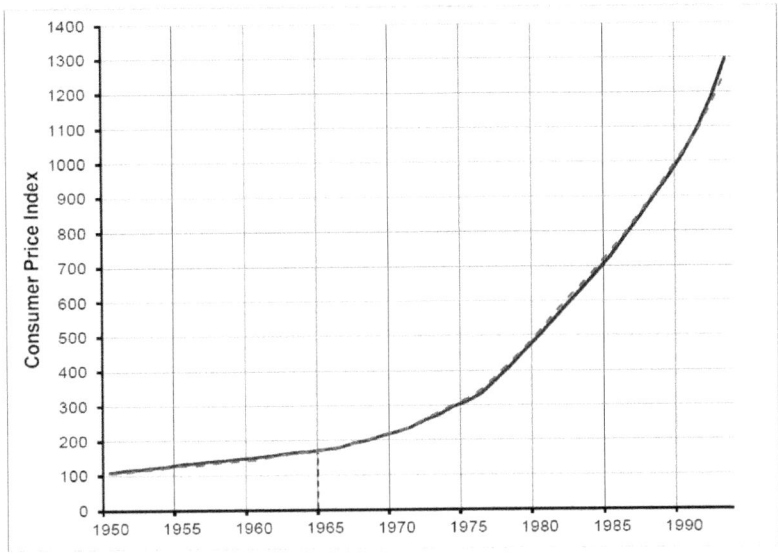

This is an indexed comparison of inflation of Total Medical Prices (-) and Physician Services (- – -) from 1950 to 1993 with Base Year 1950. As you can see, prices didn't start to spike until after 1965. (Source: US Census 2013) If you listen to those who blame the doctors, you'll hear them spew that the doctors and hospitals have created the problem by creating the demand and that is not totally true. Yes, there were doctors and hospitals that were creating problems and inflating prices to profit from, but nothing like we are seeing today. Since 1965 doctors and hospitals have been too busy meeting the demands created by the government, and complying with government regulations has become an enslaving daily nightmare. So costs have skyrocketed and will continue to do so, as quantity replaces medical quality and they decide who lives and who dies.

Welcome to the new Fast Food approach to medicine! But with one gigantic difference, they are now demanding you obey the government doctors... or you could be deemed mentally ill.

Insurance and its involvement:

In a free competitive insurance market consumers want the most benefits for the lowest health care premiums. So would the Insurance companies, and self-insured employers, want to pay the lowest amount possible to the physicians and hospitals. If the health care industry was competitive at all supply levels, and not regulated by government mandate, suppliers would aggressively offer insurers competitive prices for high quality services. Insurance companies would have no problem selecting health care policies for their policyholders that encouraged them to obtain the best service they could for the lowest cost. Consumers would protect themselves from unethical providers by taking their business to those who had a good reputation and did quality work at reasonable prices without unnecessary services. In a free competitive market, providers are forced to obtain this reputation or they go out of business.

It has been proven over and over again that government is bad for consumers and bad for business once they take control, and the reason for that is because once the government takes control you lose control. There is a good article by Mike Holly that goes into detail on this subject, and that is where I got a lot of this information.

Since the healthcare take over started we have seen a steady decline in service and a steady increase in cost. Before the big takeover of healthcare in the mid 60s costs were relatively low and doctors even made house calls.

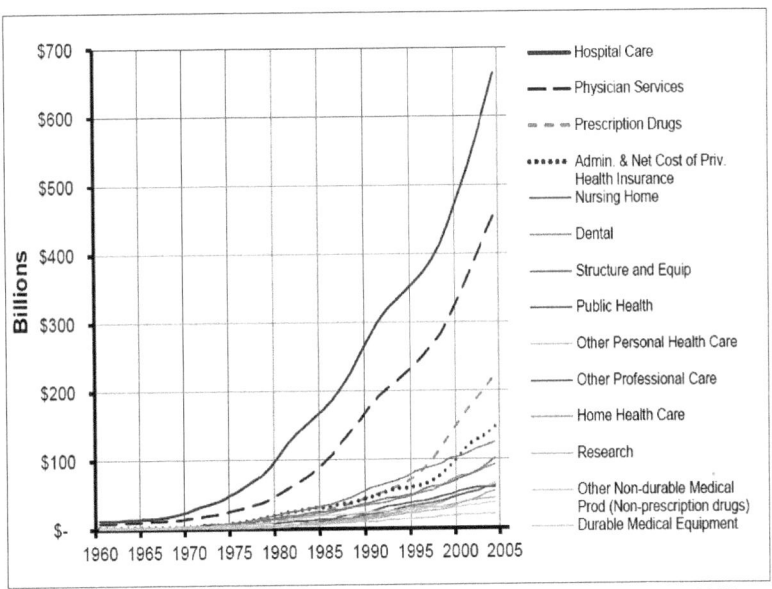

Health Care Spending in U.S. by Sector from 1960 to 2005 (Source: US Census 2013)

The following are major laws and other policies implemented by the Federal and state governments over the years that have interfered with the health care marketplace.

In 1910, the physician oligopoly was started during the Republican administration of William Taft after the American Medical Association lobbied the states to strengthen the regulation of medical licensure and allow their state AMA offices to oversee the closure or merger of nearly half of medical schools and also the reduction of class sizes. The states have been subsidizing the education of the number of doctors recommended by the AMA.

In 1925, prescription drug monopolies begun after the federal government led by Republican President Calvin Coolidge started allowing the patenting of drugs. (Drug monopolies have also been promoted by government research and development subsidies targeted to favored pharmaceutical companies.)

In 1945, buyer monopolization begun after the McCarran-Ferguson Act led by the Democrat President Roosevelt's Administration exempted the business of medical insurance from most federal regulation, including antitrust laws. (States have also more recently contributed to the monopolization by requiring health care plans to meet standards for coverage.)

In 1946, institutional provider monopolization begun after favored hospitals received federal subsidies (matching grants and loans) provided under the Hospital Survey and Construction Act passed during the Democrat President Truman's Administration. (States have also been exempting non-profit hospitals from antitrust laws.)

In 1951, employers started to become the dominant third-party insurance buyer during the Truman Administration after the Internal Revenue Service declared group premiums tax-deductible.

In 1965, nationalization was started with a government buyer monopoly after the Democrat President Johnson's Administration led passage of Medicare and Medicaid, which provided health insurance for the elderly and poor, respectively.

In 1972, institutional provider monopolization was strengthened after the Nixon Administration started restricting the supply of hospitals by requiring federal certificate-of-need for the construction of medical facilities.

In 1974, buyer monopolization was strengthened during the Nixon Administration after the Employee Retirement Income Security Act exempted employee health benefit plans offered by large employers (e.g., HMOs) from state regulations and lawsuits (e.g., brought by people denied coverage).

In 1984, prescription drug monopolies were strengthened during the Reagan Administration after the Drug Price Competition and Patent Term Restoration Act permitted the extension of patents beyond 20 years. (The government has also allowed pharmaceuticals companies to bribe physicians to prescribe more expensive drugs.)

In 2003, prescription drug monopolies were strengthened during the Bush Administration after the Medicare Prescription Drug, Improvement, and Modernization Act provided subsidies to the elderly for drugs.

In 2014, nationalization is strengthened after the Patient Protection and Affordable Care Act of 2010 ("Obamacare") forces people to have Insurance and provided mandates, subsidies and insurance exchanges, and the expansion of Medicaid.

The Government is now also working on forcing employers who reduce their employees under the number that exempts them from providing healthcare, to prove they have to downsize their labor force or prove they have to cut hours to fewer than 30, or they will not be excluded from providing healthcare insurance. The government is also working on signing laws that would make business give more people overtime. This is a major takeover of American Business just as the government took over healthcare and energy. The Fascists and Communists have done this throughout time around the world and now are doing it in America.

The Government is also working on forcing employers who are exempt from providing healthcare insurance, to request and prove their employees carry healthcare insurance before they can hire anyone. The Government is also working on making it mandatory to show proof of not only car insurance but also health insurance before you can get a drivers license or register your vehicle. You can bet this will evolve into showing proof of healthcare insurance before you get a loan or bank account or credit card, unless the American people wake up and put a stop to this anti-American tyranny.

Here is a letter that was intended to make people aware of the Real Omamcare or DemoCare:

"My name is Ashley and I'm a 26-year-old recent graduate from Michigan.

The phony Obamacare signup poster boy made me want to send a message about how Obamacare is really affecting people.

I graduated from The University of Michigan in 2009. In my state, this used to mean something, but even with a bachelor's I was told I was too educated and wouldn't stay. I watched as kids with GEDs and high school diplomas took the low-paying jobs for which I applied.

I went back to school and got a second degree and finally found work at a gym. I work nights and only get 32 hours a week for eight dollars an hour. I'm unable to find a second job at this time.

I have asthma, ulcers, and mild cerebral palsy. Obamacare takes my monthly rate from $75 a month for full coverage on my "Young Adult Plan," to $319 a month. After $6,000 in deductibles, of course.

Liberals claimed this law would help the poor. I am the poor, the working poor, and I can't afford to support myself, let alone older generations and people not willing to work at all.

This law has raped my future.

It will keep me and kids my age from having a future at all.

This is the real face of Obamacare and it isn't pretty."

I realize the USA had at one time some if not the best medical care in the world, but this you'll see will become a lot worse, and other countries will have just as good healthcare and even better than the USA. Still blows me away that this draconian law was forced on over 315,000,000 supposed free American citizens, so it could provide health insurances to 7,000,000 uninsured. Talk about a major scam on a supposed smart, free nation, this is the biggest of any I've seen. What makes this look even more pathetic is those responsible are not only still in office, but were re-elected to stay in office! Then Americans wonder why the rest of the world is laughing at America as a joke full of fools.

Medical Industry will Become a Nightmare

In 1979 Jerry Brown the governor of California hit the nail on the head, when he appeared on the Johnny Carson Show and said, "The Greatest threat to humanity is the Medical Industrial Complex, and if we don't put controls on it, they will control everyone and everything." I wasn't a fan of Moonbeam, but he sure was right on that subject.

I can tell you from what doctors tell me and what I have read in government think-tank documents, that medical care will become a real nightmare and very soon. The government and insurance companies along with big pharmaceutical companies have teamed up to control every aspect of your health. I was told by my doctor, that he couldn't practice medicine like he would like to. He told me the bureaucrats in the big medical centers and government, who have taken over of the medical field, makes it almost impossible to practice medicine and help patients on a one on one basis and to do what is best for that patient. He told me medicine has become like fast food take out... cookie cutter procedures for all patients, a one size fits all type of medical treatment. I asked him why he didn't go out on his own and start a private practice? He told me the government and big medical along with the insurance industry, would make it almost impossible to do that anymore. He said doctors are merely population controller anymore, and are basically told they better do as they are told or they will lose their license to practice if they refuse to obey. They are told what medicine they can prescribe, what procedures they can perform or order, who they can treat for whatever ails them. Any deviation from the medical menu is taboo. He also told me that in the future, the controllers of medicine and the population will be suggesting euthanasia for patients that have costly ailment that often result in death anyway... They are a financial burden on society that can be better used on those that can be saved. . I told him I read studies and documents dating back to the late 40s about the world leaders concerns with overpopulation and a need one day to cull the herd... He laughed and smiled and nodded his head yes.... He then when on to say that the medical industry is keenly aware of the overpopulation issue. He then went on to tell me that the government changed the Hippocratic Oath in the early 2000s to omit "We Swear Not To Do Any Harm" ... That is no longer in their Oath and it is because the government now allows euthanasia. Apparently the world leaders or Masters have already in place, a culling plan to thin the herd.

Overpopulation and the studies done decades ago that asked the question... "When will we have to decrease the surplus population?" Bet you didn't know they have been worried about the explosion in population, did you? In 1910, the global inhabitants was about 1.7 billion, which overwhelmingly increased in 1955 when the world had about 2.7 billion... now we have over 7.5 billion... In one of the studies, the scientists surmised that the population would exponentially increase very fast, and at 7 billion population the governments around the world start to lose control over the population and the people would lose control over the governments... At 8 billion mass migrations and gangs would invade countries and cites and the police and governments will be outnumbered and crime skyrockets. At 9 billion population, the world resources are almost depleted. Hunger and violence becomes the new normal... And at 10 billion...it is Hell on earth.

So they would have to come up with a plan to decrease the surplus population without alarming the masses. I bet you they have that plan ready now, and I am sure they will spew the biggest lie ever, and make the dumbed down masses believe that lie as they follow that black sheep to their deaths.

Here is one of their plans for your future.

OPERATION LOCKSTEP

Published in 2010

Create a Pandemic to Control

1st PHASE:

"Create or introduce an enhanced common cold/flu, (Corona Virus) that attacks people, and creates flu like complication for most people, and has a high survival rate among the healthy, but can be deadly to older people with immune deficient problems, who are a financial burden on

return life to normality. Those who have taken the vaccine will demand those who have not gotten vaccinated to get the vaccine. Doctors and hospitals will refuse to treat the unvaccinated. Many unvaccinated including children, will die from heart attacks, cancer and other treatable illnesses because the medical industry refuses to treat them. Fights will breakout between the vaccinated and unvaccinated. The government controlled healthcare industry and the vaccinated will be at war with those who have refused the vaccine. It will be anarchy from all sides... This will be the perfect time for the NWO government to step in.

Then the NWO governments around the world will declare a worldwide emergency and move in to seize total control and eliminate all resistance.

This is only one possible solution to the threat of losing control over the increasing population. We must decrease the world population, or global instability will ensue."

So they have Bio-weapons, but of course we all know that. But would they use them on the world population? One called C19, or a psychological Bio-weapon, that they will use to instill fear and a reason to create a Worldwide State of Emergency in 2019 to take global control? I am skeptical of the "Lock Step" document scenario. But, if what you have just read is true, and they are serious about decreasing the population...We should be afraid... We should be very afraid!

*****

Other interesting things to look up.

"Operation Dark Winter"

Operation Dark Winter was the code name for a senior-level bio-terrorist attack simulation conducted from June 22-23, 2001. It was designed to carry out a mock version of a covert and widespread smallpox attack on the United States.

"Agenda 21" 1992

Agenda 21 is a comprehensive plan of action to be taken globally, nationally and locally by organizations of the United Nations System, Governments, and Major Groups in every area in which human impacts on the environment.

Chapter VI

The Tightening of Control with Lies!

Inch-by-Inch it is a Synch!

Just as I foretold to a group of my friends back in 1973, when a group of friends and I were stopped in one of the first CHP Supposed Head-Light Check Points in California and asked just about every question about who we were and nothing about the headlights on the car...I told my friends that this was just the beginning and soon I saw the Gestapo would have armed road block check points and would forcibly be able to drag you out of your car and throw you to the ground, and search you and your car for no real reason, and you wouldn't be able to do a thing about it. They Laughed at me and said the people would riot! I also told people that one day the Jack Boots would be able to kick in your door without a warrant and kill your dog, beat your family to the ground and you wouldn't be able to do a thing about it... I was also laughed at and told it would never happen! Well I never saw one protest let alone a riot and everything I predicted has happened. Now the government controls every aspect of your lives, from the food and water you drink, the air you breathe,

the home you can live in, the medical care you can have, and each and every one of you who were complacent and apathetic when this was happening, is directly responsible.

The Government's Talking Points on this tyrannical takeover of our freedom was that people would do anything to stay healthy and alive! The fear of death is a great intensifier to make humans obey.

The media is a joke anymore; all have been bought off by the Orwellian Masters like George Soros, China, and Big Tech oligarchs who think they are gods. Censoring of all thought not acceptable to Big Brother and the Masters, will soon be common and those who speak out against the censoring will also be silenced. I can only guess at what diabolical nightmare the world masters will unleash on humanity to control and then thin out the herd. People are no longer needed in many industries due to machines and robots. So humans are now becoming a strain on the world resources. America has been the last bastion of freedom from total oppression and draconian rule. But that is about to change, and you aren't going to like what you see.

Once they have control over your body and organs and you can't do anything about it, you might as well consider yourselves spare parts slaves, and that day is coming! What I foresee would rival George Orwell's darkest nightmare and be the Borg's brightest Epiphany! I no doubt will be laughed at once again, but once again I will warn you of things to come! Welcome to the New Orwellian America, once you check in You Won't Be able to Check Out! There will be nowhere you can go!

First they came for the kids to teach them the government way was the only way, and none of you said anything... Then they demanded you buy health Insurance and most of you just obeyed... Then they came for the guns and none of you did anything... Then they came to put chains on you and there was no one around to say anything and it was far too late for you to do anything to stop it! So like a beaten dog slave, you just laid down and died.

Any Country that demands their citizens obey without question and force the citizens to buy anything, or demand they get medical treatments or procedures of any kind, is a Country Enslaved! And any people who believe they are free in any Country that demands they obey and force the citizens to do any of that, is a Country full of enslaved Fools!"

They Are Making a Voluntary, Mandatory!
More Lies and Deception!

In my first book; Thee Great American Illusion" I wrote about the Census Letter that came last summer claiming they were collecting data about crime and how it was "Voluntary" … Well they had sent a new letter saying they were following up and re-visiting those who didn't answer or refused the "Voluntary" request for information the first time. Oh you can bet this will get worse and far more intrusive in decades to come. And as always, the Masters will lie and the peons will probably believe the lies, because they have control of the media and they lie almost every sentence.

Sorry I digreed…. Anyway the same person who had Originally came to our door last year had returned only this time we didn't answer the door… How do I know it was the same person? I have Video and Audio Cameras around our home and I recorded this individual the last time he was here…He also left his card,… Same Person.

Well this time I didn't answer the door. He waited a while knocked again then looked directly into the camera as to let me know he knew someone was home… he left, but came back a short time later and I watched him walk around our vehicles and write something down, I asume the license plate numbers.

Since the 1st of March when this census person came back, he and another female have been back 3 more times in the month of March, 2114. Of course since I monitor video of those at my door and around our property, I let them bang on the door until they got tired and left. But each time they sat in their car and wrote a report then got on their cell phone and talked to someone. Mighty interesting don't you think? Especially hiring these people for a voluntary questionnaire. Why and what are they wasting taxpayers money for? Your Government is indeed up to something and you can bet your life it isn't something you are going to like! Our Freedom IS about to come to a Screeching Halt!

"If you tell a lie big enough and keep repeating it, people will eventually come to believe it. The lie can be maintained only for such time as the State can shield the people from the political, economic and/or military consequences of the lie. It thus becomes vitally important for the State to use all of its powers to repress dissent, for the truth is the mortal enemy of the lie, and thus by extension, the truth is the greatest enemy of the State." - Joseph Goebbels

R.W. GLESS

NCVS-573(L) LOS ANGELES
(8-2012)

UNITED STATES DEPARTMENT OF COMMERCE
Economics and Statistics Administration
U.S. Census Bureau
Washington, DC 20233-0001
OFFICE OF THE DIRECTOR

FROM THE DIRECTOR
U.S. CENSUS BUREAU

Several months ago, a representative from the U.S. Census Bureau contacted residents at your address in connection with the National Crime Victimization Survey, which the Census Bureau is conducting for the U.S. Department of Justice. We are grateful for the cooperation we were given then. The survey now calls for us to interview at your address again. Our representative needs to update the characteristics and experiences of the current residents of this address, whether we talked with you before or whether you moved to this address since our last interview.

This survey collects important information on the extent to which individuals in this country are victims of crime. The survey results are used in many ways, including by citizens to evaluate their vulnerabilities, by legislators and policymakers to develop programs to aid crime victims and prevent crime, and by researchers to understand various aspects of crime victimization.

A Census Bureau representative from our field office will contact you shortly to ask you and other members of your household some questions on this subject. We conduct this survey under the authority of Title 13, United States Code (U.S.C.), Section 8. Section 9 of this law requires us to keep all information about you and your household strictly confidential. We may use this information only for statistical purposes. Also, Title 42, Section 3732, U.S.C., authorizes the Bureau of Justice Statistics, U.S. Department of Justice, to collect information using this survey. Title 42, U.S.C., Sections 3789g and 3735, also requires us to keep all information about you and your household strictly confidential.

Because this is a sample survey, your answers represent not only you and your household, but also hundreds of other households like yours. For this reason, your participation in this voluntary survey is extremely important to ensure the completeness and accuracy of the final results. Although there are no penalties for failure to answer any question, each unanswered question substantially lessens the accuracy of the final data.

Answers to the most frequently asked survey questions are on the reverse side of this letter. If you would like further information, contact the Census Bureau by writing or calling the following office:

REGIONAL DIRECTOR
US CENSUS BUREAU
15350 SHERMAN WAY STE 400
VAN NUYS CA 91406-4203

Telephone: 1-800-992-3530

Thank you for your cooperation. The Census Bureau appreciates your help.

A Message From the Director

census.gov

I have a bad feeling that one day all of us Constitutionalist Patriots will be attacked by the Jackboots. Our homes will be raided, our pets and families murdered, because we refuse to answer questions and do not submit to warrant-less searches from any government employees. Of course that will be a good day to die fighting tyranny, but sadly the government-controlled media will spew bogus lies and make people like us look like crazy people. They will report that the police had to kill terrorist patriots who refused to submit to a warrant-less search. When asked by the media; what evidence they had against those they murdered? The Police/Gestapo will claim they had reasonable cause to search the house because the resident refused to allow them to search the home without a Search Warrant! So if you plan on going out with your boots on, draw first and remember headshots... because they wear body armor.

I know, this sounds absurd but it is already happening now! Yes this is already become a popular ploy used by Gestapo when people refuse to allow the Gestapo to violate the people's Constitutional Rights! The sickening part is that the dumbed down brain dead sheeple believe the lies the government controlled media spew, and it is becoming another precedent that the government can use to take away more of your Constitutional Rights. Yes, "We The People" have become a threat to the government leaders. Because we believe in the Constitution and in many of our cases, we have sworn an oath to uphold and defend the Constitution against all who attack it, both foreign and domestic, and by God there are a lot of domestics in the government attacking the Constitution these days!

Did you know that the Sheriff is considered the top law enforcement official of a county? Why? Because he or she is elected directly by the people and not appointed or hired, and only the people can remove a sheriff by either recall or voting them out of office.. All other supposed law officials have been created by edict or special order from the President, or governor and by city leaders. And did you know that the Sheriff and States can refuse to obey the Federal Government? Mack/Printz v USA, the U S Supreme Court declared that the states or their political subdivisions, "are not subject to federal direction." What this means is the Sheriff or any other "Subdivisions" i.e. judges, district attorneys, police, etc, do not have to obey the Federal Government when they come into a State like Storm Troopers and demand cooperation.

James Madison had stated that; *"The local or municipal authorities form distinct and independent portions of the supremacy, no more subject, within their respective spheres, to the general authority [federal government] than the general authority is subject to them, within its own sphere."*

So we the people were supposed to have had our own States Rights under the Tenth Amendment, but inch-by-inch that was handed over to the Federal Government. How did this happen? That is an easy question to answer, we allowed it to happen. The question should be; who is in the control of the Federal Government now since obviously we the people aren't?

Who is in command?

If you want to know who is controlling the government all you need to do is follow the money. The America Government is always using war to defuse the people, and get their attention off their agenda to totally control them, and controlling the government is the corporations. In the 50s and 60s you used to see Gas Wars that were attempts by oil companies to get your business. Then in the 70s the oil corporations started warring with each other and the Great Oil Company Mergers started. Many of the Mobil Gas Stations became Enco then Exxon in the Mobil/Exxon pre-merger. Then in 1999 when the merger was official it created the biggest corporation in the world. But what is the most interesting thing about the Great Oil Company Mergers is that all the American Oil Corporations were all originally Standard Oil owned up until 1911, which was the largest corporation in the world at the time. In 1911 Standard Oil was broken up because it was rule an illegal monopoly. So along with other world oil barons it just recreated its self and has once again became the largest corporation. As a matter of fact, after the federal government told JD Rockefeller that Standard Oil had to be broken up…he became even richer because he owned stock in all of the spin-off companies…

So who is controlling our governments? Yep….the corporations and many of the wars are being created by large corporation who couldn't convince the leaders of those countries to work with them. Syria is a classic example of the corporate power that controlled America. The Oil Corporations wanted to build a pipeline through Syria and the Syrian President wouldn't work with them, so they convinced their dupes in the American Government to somehow threaten Syria into submission. Yea, I know, that hasn't worked well for them yet.

Most of the Left and Right elected people in Washington have been paid off directly or through a straw donation by the Saudi Prince Bandar bin Sultan one of the richest oil barrens in the world and paid of by Big Tech also. Senators like Harry

Reid, John McCain, Lindsey Graham, Dianne Feinstein, Barbara Boxer, Robert Menendez and House Speaker John Boehner, Minority Leader Nancy Pelosi, House Intelligence Committee Chair Mike Rogers, New York's Peter King, Minority Whip Steny Hoyer, and many others have been paid in campaign contribution through Bandar, Facebook's CEO, Twitter's CEO, Amazon's Jeff Bezos and even Google! George Soros even contributes to politicians to get them elected according to several reports available on the Internet.

The henchmen of the corporate government control are the judges; they are the real traitors of freedom. It amazes me when I see blame going to the wrong group when the real blame needs to be aimed at the courts who rule against the constitution and freedom.

It is a sad fact that most have no conception of what it takes to be free. The Libertarians, Democrats and Republicans speak of peaceful rebellion to change government and that is the biggest smoke up your backside lie any enslaved group could ever spew! Those who have too much cowardice to fight for their freedom are bound to enslavement! Freedom is worth dying for and those who aren't willing to die to be free aren't worth listening to. If you really want to be free, you must be willing to die for it. Otherwise you might as well just shut up and cower in your illusionary safe place under your bed, in the cage your master, the government has created for you, and hope a peaceful rally will free you one day. You see how that works for you. Those in power got there by fighting to get there, and they did it by force, and no other way will get them out. We have to take to the streets to stop the culling of freedom and man. You can't just bitch at your TV as you sit in your easy chair and expect things to get better, it aint gonna happen! Now when I say take to the Streets, I mean get up and out and convince people that there is a pending doom and rally the masses to throw the bums out before it comes to violent war!

We The People should have the same power as the Government and we should have the same exemption if we defend ourselves against tyrannical Government/Gestapo! If attacked by a tyrant we should defend ourselves with any force necessary to protect ourselves and the lives of our families! But unfortunately we allowed the Right we had under the Bill of Right, Second Amendment, to be eroded away and now we will be killed by the government if we defend ourselves against their tyranny. Can you say Police State?

Now I hear tell, not that I would know, (lol) that there are insurance plans you can get in South America that start out at $250,000 and up as high as you can afford that stipulates that if you are killed/murdered, to anyone who makes sure all involved are brought to "Justice" they will receive the money. Note: "Justice" is loosely defined! And they must show proof! i.e. those responsible in jail or a death certificate and you are the one who avenged the insured. This will ensure you are not murdered in vain and anyone who kills you "period" including Gestapo will be dealt with accordingly, and hopefully they will have no place on the face of planet they can hide! Now if this is true, then that is a true international post mortem health insurance policy... Don't you think?

It is amazing to think this all started well over 100 years ago. What is the amazing part is that while the communist movement was growing in Russia and China, the people oppressed over there were coming to America to be freer. Now Russia is moving away from communism and into a more capitalist society and America is moving into a Communist society like China. It is like the American people have been asleep for the last 100 years and hadn't been watching the demise of Communism in Europe and how it hadn't worked. Or Americans are all junkies who just don't care as long as they get their government fix of free-bees... At any cost, freedom, health, self worth, pride, life and happiness, none of that matters as long as they get their government free-bee dope that they have become addicted too! I guess I have to consider that "Just Say No To Drugs" didn't work and can only be as naive to think "Just Say No To Total Government Control" will work? Dependency is a very hard Drug Habit to get over and the Government knows this too well. They have had centuries perfecting and domesticating the citizens into dependent farm animals with little or no will to be free again. Luckily there are still those of us with the wild animal still in us that will never ever be truly domesticated.

We have to fight to get our freedom back and there is no doubt in my mind that many of us who believe in freedom will be killed and murdered by the new American Gestapo, but it is better to die fighting tyranny than to live enslaved under it! Just please don't die cowering like a beaten slave, die fighting standing up for freedom and taking as many of the enemy as you can with you! The American People are being targeted by the government and it is a War as far as they are concerned, so you better accept the fact that we are under siege and prepare!

******

Chapter VII

Global Anomalies & Other Diversions

You are probably wondering what global anomalies have to do with the American enslavement. Well, a lot! Government has been boring tunnels underneath our feet for years, literally, and playing with our atmosphere, our food and our genetic make-up, and more importantly, our minds. We are all just a cash cow labor force for government revenue generation, and they need a way to keep us enslaved. What better way to do this than to create and control mini-disasters and make you believe that the only help for these mini-disasters is the government?

Sinkholes, floods, storms, disease are increasing in severity and frequency, and you could chalk it up to natural anomalies, and in many cases you'd be right. But not all cases are naturally occurring. Many are indeed man made and not from the bogus global warming either. Just as finances and the Stock Market are rigged, so are many of the global crisis and global anomalies, and wars. It's all about control folks, plain and simple, your control and obedience. Yet most Americans keep believing the lies that their "Con-manders and Thief's" continue to spew!

Let's look at the conflicts that the American government gets into in the Middle East. None have been anything but a nightmare and failure. You hear the excuses by military leaders and elected officials alike. But no one ever seems to notice the time the media and the people spend talking about it and the massive resources the government spends on it. Could it be that these crises are deliberately created and not the result of bungling fools in power, as we are lead to think? It would benefit those in power to keep the American people's mind off the out of control government corruption, and benefit those who build and create weapons of war, now wouldn't it?

Your government also has frequency weapons that can create havoc on you and your surroundings. These frequency weapons are both audio and electrical. Sometimes they are combined, sometimes they aren't. Audio weapons are different than electrical weapons, audio weapons are like those uses by police and military, which send out a low or high frequency to disperse protester. Electrical frequency weapons use high or low voltage frequencies at different amps to disable not only the living, but also just about anything, machines, homes, water, air, you name it! With an electrically charged frequency weapon, that combines audio and electrical frequency, that has enough amperage and concentration, you can bring down a mountain or create a title wave capable of wiping out anything along a coastline.

When I was heavily into the electronics business in the 80s and early 90s, we experimented with frequency. At the time I was also a Contractor for the Federal Government…. Yeah one of those spooky people… We were heavily into audio and speaker design as well as radio frequency stuff. I was also interested in ion power and created a little ion generator that would float a paper straw craft around the table. That is when I got interested in what frequency could do.

I had done work for different federal agencies and had tech talks with several of the people who would hire me to (Fix a Problem) for them… Then out of the blue, one day an older gentleman had come in to talk with me about an invention he was working on and ask if I would be interested in teaming up with him to develop it. I was intrigued when he told me about his ideas, so I was in. His name was Cliff and he had created a frequency-boring tool, or I should say he was in the process of modifying a dental frequency drill that was able to bore a 15 thousand perfect round hole in selenium substrate material.

It was basically a transducer and a hollow surgical needle that was tuned to a specified frequency that equaled the resonating frequency of whatever we wanted to bore a hole in. There was a slurry abrasive that was used also, and we were able to bore a perfectly round hole through a quarter inch in less than three minutes.

Now for those of you who don't know what selenium substrate is? It is a condensed rock like material that can withstand high heat used in electronic applications and other industrial applications. So creating a way to machine it was a big deal in the 80s and early 90s, back when we were experimenting with it.

Now the reason I bring this up is because the engineer that I was working with was one of the government engineers that helped create a faster way to product cold rolled steel in the 40s, and he was in his late 70s at the time. He had me designing the electronics and he would do most of the testing. I knew the frequencies we were dealing with, at the power levels coupled with the transducer... should be shielded, or whom-ever used it should be shielded, but engineer Cliff scoffed it off saying I was too paranoid. But I can tell you this, that darn thing made my skin crawl whenever I was with in a foot or so of it, and I knew we needed to shield the transducer at least. But since we were in the R&D stages and testing several different transducers that we made on site with a lathe, and Cliff was in a hurry to get it perfected because he had a potential company investor back east who was funding the research.

He didn't believe there was any problem or harm the frequencies could do and disregarded my safety concerns regarding the resonate frequencies. Then low and behold a leaded shield miraculously appeared at our back loading door one morning, which apparently was from the military judging from the grey paint and number on it....It had a little leaded window, and was on rollers like the kind you see in X-Ray Rooms... I was and still am, indeed grateful to whoever supplied it. After months of testing Cliff came into the shop and said he wasn't feeling well and was going to the doctor to get some tests done. He was in his 80s after all, so I figured that at his age the doctor would probably tell him to start taking it easy. About a week later he came in and told me he had developed cancer. He had it everywhere even in his brain. I immediately, said I knew that he should have shielded himself around that damn thing, but he scoffed it off and said it wasn't from the machine, he thought it was from the work he did in WWII developing faster cold rolled steel production and the exposure to toxins they had worked with including asbestos. I however believed otherwise, and still do! He had been working on that boring machine for a year before we teamed up, so his exposure to it had lasted years.

Even though it was low voltage and a low amperage tabletop-boring unit, and we never got any microwave radiation detected off the unit, I would always use the windowed lead shield after realizing its potentially damaging resonating frequency radiation. When the unit was on not boring into anything, it didn't bother me, but once it started boring a hole I could feel the frequency it resonated. After Cliff died the project was scraped or so I was informed ... but I think the government has one perfected to its utmost potential now.

I am telling you this story so you can get an idea of the potential power of Frequency and what it can do, and what it has done! Ironically years later I too developed cancer but luckily it was cut out and so far no more has been detected.

Now imagine what the government and military have been playing with over the years. They have basically an unlimited budget if they see a potential weapon or tool they can use, and there is no doubt that they have play-toys that would pop your mind like a champagne cork.

Earthquakes and Volcanoes

You're going to see a lot more Earthquakes and Volcanoes in places that never had any, and in places that have never had any. And the information that we the people used to be able to get to detect the possibility of them, are now being hidden or not subject to public information anymore. We are seeing activity in the west and east, in American, that never been recorded before, and your government is making less and less of the information available. Why? Because they want to stop the reality of a major earth shaking volcanic problems from the public so they can use it to the government's advantage! How? To control you!

Some say a lot of these anomalies are caused by our government. Our government is building deep under ground bases that go for miles, and some of those subterranean facilities maybe right under your feet! DARPA is but one of many quasi civilian/military organization involved in experimental research.

Oh and the Bio Weapons you will be infected with in the future is going to be a real culling event... A final way to get you totally enslaved and obedient.

Open Your Mind and Stop Falling Prey to Diversions

Stop buying into the news diversions that divert your attention from the real problem of government abuse. You have to be aware of the diversion that crops up every time a government problem or embarrassment becomes daily conversation on the Internet or in the media. Planes missing, weather anomalies, or Putin and Russian issues that have absolutely nothing to do with you, or absolutely will do nothing to you or for you!

All the media outlets play the diversion game and sadly people keep buying into it and taking their eye off the real enemy and real disaster that will and does directly affect them... The Government's seizing of your freedom and financing! It has become pathetic to the point that it is hard to believe people are thinking for themselves at all! Like automatons marching in a lock step goose march without the slightest idea of what is going on.

I am laughing at the once free Country called America

crying over the Russians taking charge of their own destiny, and I have to say I think Putin is a far better President than America has seen in their own Country in years. The guy doesn't mess around and takes care of business...Maybe he should fake a U.S. birth certificate and run for President in the U.S?...He'd probably get elected, and maybe then we would secure our borders and stop the criminals flooding into the U.S.

America as a free nation is over anyway because the brain dead keep voting in mentally handicapped people like Pelosi who are so out of touch with reality... they should be in a home for the mentally handicapped. Or that dummy senator from Texas of all places that think the constitution is not valid because it is over 400 years old.

America has become a laughing stock, and a lot of people think of Americans as morons across the world, and the funniest part is the dopy people in this country don't care how stupid other people think they are or how owned they are... But I guess that is pretty obvious since they keep voting in idiots that should be mentally evaluated or at least have to prove they done grad-gee-ated the 6 grade like Jethro Bodine.... It is so pathetic it is sickening and just adds to the destruction of our freedom and our enslavement.

So...Who really owns you? Well the protectioneers ... yep just like the gangsters who offer protection; only they are now your government, healthcare and the insurance companies who own the government. Think about it... you have to have insurance for everything, and now the government is forcing and demanding you pay for bogus taxes and insurance by threat of fines and in some instances imprisonment. So you are basically being strong-armed by the very government that you are supposed to control. Even with headlines of corrupt officials like San Francisco's State Assemblyman Leland Lee. Who spews the gun control that all the other leftist spew... "No citizen should own guns!", who was under arrest for setting up a gun and weapons buy to an under cover FBI agent for rocket launchers and machine guns. Some of you still vote these crooks into office This Democrat poster child, Leland Lee, was also demanding pay-offs for political favors and protection according to what he was charged with. Want to bet real money this will be silently reported or omitted by the fascist/leftist media? No...didn't think so.

****

Orwellian Fascist and Socialists Promise they can change the plight of a depressed people. Normally they come to power after a country's economy crashes and or some other national catastrophe or panned-demic. They always promise the same things. Safety and Security… And the people always get the same thing…Enslavement!

Useful idiots, are the leftists who are idealistically believing in the beauty of the Soviet socialist or Communist or whatever system, but when they get disillusioned, they become the worst enemies.- Vladimir Lenin

Chapter VIII

YOU OWN NOTHING IN AMERICA!

Under the forfeiture laws you own nothing! And Americans say little or nothing about it... let alone do anything to stop it!

What is even worse is the Government can seize anything you own and there is little you can do about it. Police steal billions of dollars of seizes property every year and it can be bank accounts, cars, money, jewelry and even your house! All they have to say is you are suspected of being a criminal, and they don't even have to charge you with a crime! Oh you can try and fight them but once they take everything you own, how are you going to pay an attorney to fight the tyrants? They own the printing press and own the courts... So good luck fighting that Tyranny.

Americans are suppose to be innocent until proven guilty in a court of law, but we all know that is a joke on us especially under the civil forfeiture laws that make you guilty until proven innocent. Under the Civil Forfeiture Law the police/Gestapo can steal any or all of your personal property merely because they say it may have been obtained through criminal activity. It was originally used by the British in America in the 1700s to seize ships and their content that didn't fly the British Flag. The British law required any ship transporting goods from a British port had to fly the British flag and of course to do that you had to pay a tax to the crown. Ships that were caught flying any other flag were subject to attack and the ship, crew and cargo seized and forfeit. This was done because the owners of the ships were normally not on the ships used to transport goods and therefore the British couldn't arrest and seize the owner's total wealth, so they would take what they could from them, which was their ship, cargo and crew. This was used as a tool in the Revolutionary War against America, and unfortunately was parroted by the U.S. Congress as a model for the first American Forfeiture Laws aimed at customs revenue, which was about 90% of the Government's funding at the time. It was supposed to be used against those braking maritime law and not paying duty tax when it was almost impossible to arrest the owner or kingpin who was breaking the law. Now this "maritime law" tool use to combat crime and tax evasion has been perverted into any illegal or supposed illegal activity, and the police/Gestapo routinely use this to fund their army and buy equipment used against you the common citizens... There is no reasonable cause involved. If the local Gestapo were to take a disliking to you, they could claim you gained your home and cars and other personal property by illegal activity and seize it all. The odds on you being able to get it back is slim and none since they don't actually have to prove you did anything illegal, just claim they believe you had, or plant some incriminating evidence against you. The new ISM is Terrorism or terrorist that they use on Americans.

In 1984 the Department of Justice created the Asset Forfeiture Fund, and in the second year 1986 after its creation Department of Justice took in $93.7 million in proceeds from forfeited assets. After they realized this was a gold mine to collect a fortune without having to justify stealing it, the amount in 2008 skyrocketed to more than $1 billion in forfeited assets. It no doubt has risen since then with more and more agencies taking advantage of these free stolen goods and cash they now can easily take from you. Once again this goes back to your 4th, 5th, 6th and 8th Amendments that have been ignored.

Property Tax: There are no states in America anymore that don't require you pay property tax. So in

essences, you really don't own your home or business, you rent is from the government.

Property tax varies from state to state but it is basically a luxury tax. So if you don't pay the taxes imposed on property you own, after a set time, normally several years of unpaid property taxes, the government can seize your property and you forfeit your property and basically lose it. Again, we are all guilty of allowing this to happen, and it is really sad when some old couple in their 70 or 80s living on a fixed income lose their home because they can't afford to pay the government tax imposed on them. They have to either go live with a relative or go into an old folk's home and in some cases are forced out into the streets only to die shortly thereafter. A lot of states now just put a lien on old people's property and when they die they sell it and get the back tax and penalties, but it is still a sad commentary for a country that claims to be free. I believe people over 70 should be exempt from all taxes but the government will never allow that to happen.

Death Tax i.e. Estate Tax

Sounds like a nightmare from the grave but Americans are taxes for everything even in death. Here is the definition from the IRS web page. What the definition doesn't explain is it can be as high as 55%...better than half of everything you own, especially after you factor in attorneys.

Estate Tax or Death Tax as defined by the IRS

"The Estate Tax is a tax on your right to transfer property at your death. It consists of an accounting of everything you own or have certain interests in at the date of death. The fair market value of these items is used, not necessarily what you paid for them or what their values were when you acquired them. The total of all of these items is your "Gross Estate." The includible property may consist of cash and securities, real estate, insurance, trusts, annuities, business interests and other assets.

Once you have accounted for the Gross Estate, certain deductions (and in special circumstances, reductions to value) are allowed in arriving at your "Taxable Estate." These deductions may include mortgages and other debts, estate administration expenses, property that passes to surviving spouses and qualified charities. The value of some operating business interests or farms may be reduced for estates that qualify.

After the net amount is computed, the value of lifetime taxable gifts (beginning with gifts made in 1977) is added to this number and the tax is computed. The tax is then reduced by the available unified credit.

Most relatively simple estates (cash, publicly traded securities, small amounts of other easily valued assets, and no special deductions or elections, or jointly held property) do not require the filing of an estate tax return. A filing is required for estates with combined gross assets and prior taxable gifts exceeding $1,500,000 in 2004 - 2005; $2,000,000 in 2006 - 2008; $3,500,000 for decedents dying in 2009; and $5,000,000 or more for decedent's dying in 2010 and 2011 (note: there are special rules for decedents dying in 2010); $5,120,000 in 2012, $5,250,000 in 2013 and $5,340,000 in 2014.

Beginning January 1, 2011, estates of decedents survived by a spouse may elect to pass any of the decedent's unused exemption to the surviving spouse. This election is made on a timely filed estate tax return for the decedent with a surviving spouse. Note that simplified valuation provisions apply for those estates without a filing requirement absent the portability election."

I realize that millions in assets is a lot of assets, but to have to pay upwards of 55% is outrageous since you are forfeiting over half of all you have acquired in your lifetime. If you have... let's say an Apartment Building or Hotel, and your family lives there and helps run the place, and it is let's say worth 6 million and you own it cash flat out. But it only makes enough to pay the property tax, utilities, and maintenance, with enough left over to supports your family... If you die, they are forced to come up with over 3 million in taxes or they are out on the streets. This scenario happened to a family in New York City several years ago and it didn't seem fair then and doesn't seem fair now. I realize they probably should have formed a corporation and divided it equally before the father's death, but he didn't and the kids wound up losing over 3 million and the home/hotel that had been in the family for decades...all because of the Death or Estate Tax. So you aren't even free in death in America anymore especially if you are among those who have made new money or have old money. It is probably in your best interest to invest your money in a country that doesn't steal it from you if you die... if of course, you are among those in the dough.

Now for all us poorer folk we may not have to worry about the Federal Death/Estate Tax but we very well may have to deal with a STATE Death/Estate Tax and that is a much lower asset value. Here are the States that collect a Death/Estate Tax; Connecticut, Delaware, District of Columbia, Hawaii, Illinois, Maine, Maryland, Massachusetts, Minnesota, New Jersey, New York, Oregon, Rhode Island, Tennessee (Until 2016), Vermont, Washington.

Need more proof? How about this. A man in Indiana in his 90s had been collecting artifacts from around the world for over 80 years, since he was a little kid, and some snotty brown nosing jerk saw all of these treasures and calls the federal government and tells them this guy has historic relics he shouldn't have and the damn government raids this old man's home and seize everything. This old man collected most of this before these snotty nosed punks were even born and long before any laws were ever passed against owning relics. Doesn't matter to the government! They make up the rules as they go or to suit their needs! The government's excuse is that the relics have to have been stolen... yea right. If the government told me it was sunny outside I wouldn't believe them, and I'd have to go look for myself. That is how much I distrust the American government today. I don't believe a word they say, because the government is a bold faced liar.

Eminent Domain: Eminent Domain is a way the

government uses to take your property without your consent. It happens all the time in every state in America. The government decides it wants your property to benefit their revenue base in some way and, Poof; you no longer are the owner. Of course the government will give you "Fair Market Value" whatever they decide that might be, but you are still the victim of a hostile takeover.

Case in point: A couple in Colorado, Andy and Ceil Barrie own a cabin surrounded by forest land and the Fed said they were disturbing the nature when they used the old logging road that was built to get to their property. So they told the couple they couldn't use the road to get to their property. This didn't bode well with the couple so they went to the county and showed the county that they used to maintain that road so they ask the county to declare it a county road. Now that pissed off the Fed big time and they leaned on the county with some heavy weight and cut a deal with the county. The Fed had land in town that could be developed into a commercial site that would bring in needed tax revenue. But, the Fed needed something in return....yep they wanted the couples cabin and land, and the county could impose eminent domain on the couples cabin and property and seize it, then swap it for the Fed's property. Sweet deal for the government, wasn't it? But the couple loved their cabin and land and fought the seizer. They were threaten and told they couldn't fight the government and some of the corporate medias reported the story, but they too reported it as if it was a losing battle.

The culprit in this case is Summit County, Colorado, which refused interview requests from the media, and instead released a statement saying: *"Both parties engaged in productive negotiations in pursuit of a voluntary settlement regarding the purchase. ... We are optimistic that a resolution will be reached within a matter of weeks, if not days."* Yea, right by stealing property from the Barrie's like you see in those old western land barron movies, where the gang of thugs threaten the land owner into selling to the land barron or else! So once again you merely rent property from the government and if they decide they want to break your lease, slash, supposed ownership, they can and you are S.O.L.

Mark these words! I strongly believe in the future the government will make you upgrade your home under the guise that it was built with substander materials that cause health issues. They will force home owners to totally remodel and reinsulate with new "Government Aproved" materials every 10 or so years, and if you don't they will condemn and impose Eminent Domain and take your home claiming it was a health hazard to humanity. It will be a total lie but the mindless masses will just bah bah bah along with it like the sheeple they are, totally oblivious to the fact that it is blatant revenue generation for the government. If you comply it equals revenue and if you refuse and they take it from you, it still equals revenue for the government because everything you do that requires money equals taxes! Either Sales Tax or Income Tax, that is the sad simple truth and the travesty we the people have allowed to enslave us all.

Here is the real truth, and many of you will once again call me an extremist, but facts are facts. You don't even own yourself anymore! Nope, the government owns you and now that you get fined for not obeying your master/owner the government if you refuse to pay for healthcare, your are indeed owned just for being born and now have to pay to be alive! Oh I know a few of you will try and say that I don't have to pay them anything, and you don't, but they will fine you and even if at present the government isn't placing any liens on your property. But you wait until this healthcare law gets past the possibility of being appealed. Then you mark my words good! Your house, car, salary, and anything they can take from you including your freedom by threat of imprisonment, will become a lien reality!

****

"Any Country that demands their citizens obey and force the citizens to buy anything, or do something against their will, is a Country Enslaved!

And any people who believe they are free in any Country that demands they obey and force the citizens to buy anything, or do anything against their will, is a Country of Fools!" – R.W. Gless.

Chapter VIIII

Do Americans Want To Be Free?

Do Americans want to be free, that is the question indeed! From the response given every time a freedom guaranteed in the Bill of Rights is revoked you wouldn't think so. The irony is that America has become 47th in its citizens personal freedom…47th! America used to be number 1 or first in citizen's freedom, now 47th.

You always hear those in control say there is a "Price for Freedom" or "Cost of Freedom" and just about every time they start to spew those words, you can bet you are about to lose freedom! Yet very few ever say anything against the freedom grabbers. So I have to believe that most Americans don't want to be free, they like being slaves subservient to a master that always wants more.

Here are some good examples I found on the Internet:
"Federal Government, which has the power to take you property and thanks to the patriot act without a court order. It has the power to tax without your consent. It has the power to put you in prison. We gave them the power to

regulate the horsepower of our cars so that we do not go too fast on the highway. We only gave up a little bit of our freedom for safety of our highways.

State Government, has the power to take your property. Has the power to tax you without your consent. Has the power to put you in prison. We allow the state to regulate what guns we can carry and if we are even allowed to even have a gun. After all we are only giving up a little bit of freedom for our common safety.

County Government has the power to take your property. Has the power to tax you without your consent. Has the power to put you in prison. It even has the power to tell you where you can walk in the park. After all we only are giving up a little bit of our freedom for common safety.

Zoning commissions; we allow the zoning board to tell us where to build a house and what our house should look like. After all we only are giving up a little bit of our freedom for common good.

City, Town, and Village Government, have the power to take your property. They have the power to tax you without your consent. They have the power to put you in prison. They control the quality of your water what additives go in it and how much to tax you, when you get it. They even provide the garbage police to make sure we do not put the incorrect garbage into the recycle containers. We give up a little bit of freedom to gain a little bit of good.

Public school board governments, have the power to take your property. Have the power to tax you without your consent. We give up the education of our most important assets to a few people who, in many cases, brainwash young minds and don't even teach them to read and write properly. Look at "Occupy Wall Street", as the protesters are interviewed, none of them can state why they are there, nor can they even come up with a coherent sentence. I might add many of them are collage students.

Finally we have homeowners associations. They have the power to take your property. They have the power to tax you without your consent. They have the power to tell you what plants you can have in your front or back yard. They have the power to tell you what color you can paint your door. They have the power when to tell you when to paint your door. They have the power to tell you what automobile you can have in your driveway and how long it can stay there. They have the power to tell you how long an automobile can stay in front of your house. You cannot buy a house in any development without submitting to the regulations of a HOA. We give up a LOT of freedom so that we do not have that purple house next door, a little bit of security.

With all of these rules and regulations of a homeowners association, why are we complaining about the federal telling we must wear out seat belts? Why do we complain about Michelle Obama trying to tell us what we should have for breakfast and how big our portions should be? Why do we complain about Obama wanting to regulate the temperature in our living rooms? We say, we want freedom yet we want a constitutional amendment to tell us whom we can marry, oh I mean who the other person can marry. We say we want freedom, but we want an amendment to tell us whom we cannot vote for, called term limits.

We, as Americans, say we want freedom, but we willingly give up freedom for a little bit of security in every level of government, that we have willingly inflicted upon ourselves. We, as Americans, have the government we so willingly give to ourselves. We, as Americans, have the government we purchase each and every day. We, as Americans, have willingly purchased our tyranny we live under all in the name of a little bit of safety. Ben Franklin once said; 'They who can give up essential liberty to obtain a little temporary safety deserve neither liberty nor safety'. We as Americans have the government we deserve. Therefore I ask again, do we, as Americans, really want to be free? Until we decide that we want to be free at all levels of government, including the most pernicious HOAs, we will never be free. Therefore, to say that we want freedom is a total hoax that we are willingly perpetrating on ourselves." - John A. Rosado

The above also ties into the fact that you own nothing in America and maybe should have been placed in that chapter, but it also speaks to the lack of will of the people to want to be free.

Lie after lie has been told to take our freedom, and time after time the American people allow their government to lie repeatedly again and again to them. IRS gets caught targeting anyone who believes in the Constitution then tells the people and Congress to screw off. Then by some stroke of fate all the evidence on the hard drives of the head of the IRS, Lois Lerner, coincidently is destroyed,...and like a sheep caught in the headlights of an oncoming semi, the mindless masses just look at these lies stupefied and do nothing, just stand there with a blank look on their faces. Then the liars involved in directing the IRS to target Constitutionalists, i.e. the socialists and communists, come up for re-election and the people re-elect them! Unbelievable!

We are conditioned to believe we live in a Country of Laws. But things have changed in our belief that no one is above those laws. I often hear people say that only the common people have to obey the laws and none of the officials are paying any attention to laws protecting the common people... surely not the lawmakers and law enforcers. They have totally ignored the Constitution and our Bill of Rights and some have even outspokenly said they want to change the Bill of Rights and take out several Amendments leaving only 5 or 6.

I realize we can't live in this country for free, but to have to give up everything we own including ourselves isn't freedom. It is surely not what the founding Fathers had in mind when they fought the law of England to make us free from oppression, tax abuse, and slavery. War and possible death or being taxed into enslavement was their choices they had to ponder, and they chose war and treason against England. As far as they were concerned it was the lesser of the two evils to revolt against the law and commit treason against the government to gain freedom, than to remain oppressed and enslaved.

There is a known legal philosophy called "The Lesser of two evils", or "Choice of Evils Defense" which is a defense to a criminal charge based on the assertion that the criminal act was committed to avoid the commission of an even greater evil. According to this defense a defendant should be exculpated even if they have caused harm or an evil which would ordinarily constitute a criminal offense, if the defendant has not caused a net harm or evil because of justifiable circumstances. Not all States and jurisdictions recognize this defense and less and less of the courts are allowing it. In those jurisdictions that recognize the choice of evils defense, it encompasses both of the older defenses of duress and necessity. Example of this would be if you have a person in your car having a heart attack and there is no time to wait for help so you speed to the hospital to save that persons life. Or if you or someone else is being attacked by an animal like a bear or large dog and that animal will kill the person it is attacking, and you get you gun and shoot and kill that animal. Even if there is a law that makes discharging a weapon in that area or the animal is on some endangered list, it was a Lesser of Two Evils situation.

Choice of Evils Defense is also known as lesser-evils defense or general-justification defense, and those courts that refuse to allow this defense are in no way courts that believe in your freedom, or well being.

It is too bad that most people don't take extreme prejudges when they see a judge blatantly spit on a defendants Rights and side with law enforcers that have blatantly abused the Rights of that defendant. Instead of starting a Recall if allowed, or demanding that Judge be taken off the bench, most people will just shrug their shoulders and say they can't fight the government. That is in no way freedom! That is the mark of a beaten people that are totally enslaved!

It also isn't freedom when we have allowed those we elect to dictate to us when we are supposed to be dictating to them. After all, aren't "We the People" supposed to be in charge of our elected leaders, not the other way around? It's too bad that the majority of the people don't care about freedom anymore. I for one cannot live happily oppressed and enslaved and would rather die fighting for my freedom. That is why I am writing these books, in hope that other who feel as I do, will stand up and say something before we can't say anything. Unfortunately for people like myself who knew the freedom we once had and have lost, the government will probably sooner or later have to get rid of us because we stand in the way of total government domination over you.

I have to mention the media once again, who are the propaganda outlets for the government. Because too many people believe the obvious spin and attempt to subliminally implant their ideals. All of the medias do this both Right and Left, and it has become so blatant it is amazing to me that more people can't see it. CNN even had a commentator say this blatantly anti-freedom statement; *"I think the American people, honestly, want security over freedom."- Jake Tapper CNN.* On Fox News those in the opposite camp were screaming for the head of Edward Snowden for exposing the government's blatant disregard for the Constitution. They spew that Snowden is a traitor. If that is the case, then what is the government agency that is spying illegally on the citizen in direct violation of the Constitution?

Even when a President basically tells the people they don't deserve to be free, the mindless masses still don't see the threat to freedom. In 2013 President Obama basically told a Kansas audience that very thing in a speech he gave. I will just quote a part of that speech that has been a source of controversy:

"There is a certain crowd in Washington who, for the last few decades, have said, let's respond to this economic

challenge with the same old tune. "The market will take care of everything," they tell us. If we just cut more regulations and cut more taxes–especially for the wealthy– our economy will grow stronger. Sure, they say, there will be winners and losers. But if the winners do really well, then jobs and prosperity will eventually trickle down to everybody else. And, they argue, even if prosperity doesn't trickle down, well, that's the price of liberty.

Now, it's a simple theory. And we have to admit, it's one that speaks to our rugged individualism and our healthy skepticism of too much government. That's in America's DNA. And that theory fits well on a bumper sticker. (Laughter.) But here's the problem: It doesn't work. It has never worked. (Applause.) It didn't work when it was tried in the decade before the Great Depression. It's not what led to the incredible postwar booms of the '50s and '60s. And it didn't work when we tried it during the last decade. (Applause.) I mean, understand, it's not as if we haven't tried this theory." – President Obama

It is the last paragraph that speaks volumes when he says freedom or the free market doesn't work. That should have been a soul chilling revelation to anyone who believes in freedom who was really listening. What is even more soul chilling is the thought that those applauding were listening and believe Americans don't deserve to be free and need government control over them.

I realize that being a Constitutionalist Patriot that sees through the BS is a threat to the government. They known that we know, that the people have allowed them to grow into a dictatorship, just as it was when another group of Americans woke up and decided it was better to die fighting for their freedom than to be enslaved by a government way out of control. I believe we have to defy those who threaten our freedom by introducing laws to further enslave us, then hiding behind their position of legal power to justify their tyranny.

****

Do you remember the Milkman?

Do you remember the Helms Bakery Truck?

Do You remember only having a Black & White TV?

If you remember these things then you remember an America that was much freer than it is today.

Chapter X

Redefining Reality

Humans are chronic liars and will continue to be liars and manipulate the truth to suit its own wants and needs. They redefine words and other truths to convince others and gain control over others. Let me give you an example; lets say God had said to man that the color white was always to be likened to holy honest truth. Well it would only be a matter of time before some leader, dictator or government control nut or nuts try and convince everyone that the color white isn't really white it is really red and that God really meant the color red was a Holy color. You would say, "No it is not!" Red is Red! It is not White or any other color but RED! And they would tell you that science and the law has redefined the Color White to really be RED and you better get used to it or you will face arrest. Most of the people would just obey and Red would become the new White.

This is the same way those who want you totally enslaved have told you that limiting your Constitutional Rights isn't really limiting any of your Rights, because they have redefined what those Constitutional Rights really are. NO...

the Right to Bear Arms doesn't mean you can own a gun....No Sir! It really means you only have the Right if the Government Grants it to You! NO...you don't have the Right to refuse a government order, like buying a product from Insurance Companies or any other company deemed Royal by the Government, because they have redefined what Freedom really means. White is no longer White as God has says because God never really said the color white was White. Air isn't really clear it is Dark a Pitch! Your eyes just see Black as Clear, and therefore clear is really black as pitch. Yes, I know, just another form of Social Engineering, and mind control, but I was trying to make the point a littler clearer for you....or wait, darker, or …. Oh never mind!

A great example of an American leader "Redefining Reality" was Franklin D. Roosevelt who was a Progressive and believed that the task of politicians is to redefine our rights and in his own words; "in the terms of a changing and growing social order." Our Founders thought the truths they celebrated in the Declaration of Independence were self-evident and were to be timeless and unchanging. But FDR wanted and argued for a new self-evident economic truth. His proposed "Economic Bill of Rights" laid out the means to create our new economic rights and how they are to be secured to achieve social equality and social justice.

Social Equality and Social Justice were merely sound good buzzwords for a new American Socialism, and was the beginning of the end for American Freedom, and the start of the entitlement age. It was a way for the government to control just about every aspect of your lives. So FDR created his Second Bill Of Rights to expand and circumvent the original Bill of Rights into his vision of Social Equality and Social Justice or his new Socialist Order. FDR was a student and master in Progressive Ideals and how through "Redefining" truths he could change America into what he envisioned.

So you need to be as clever as those who control you. If you are told you are being anti-government, you have to tell them no you are pro-freedom and that is pro-government and they are traveling under a false definition because being anti-government and tyranny isn't anti-government or even seditious. No way! It is being Pro-Constitution and Pro-Freedom! Therefore only those in government who lie to the people and try and convince the citizens that anyone who questions those in government are anti-government, are really the seditious and traitorous ones. Just as those who try and tell you that God didn't really mean White was White and will terminate anyone who refuses to except the new White is Red, you have to spin it back at them! Am I making any sense to you? It is a devilish mind game that has totally stupefied mankind and made mankind a slave and the majority of them mental midgets! In short what I am saying is you need to tell these liars in office; "Don't piss down my back and tell me it's raining!"

I am going to leave you with this little slice of reality. I had this in closing my last book but I have changed it to fit today's situation, and if ever a speech was as true then, it is more so true now.

"No man thinks more highly than I do of the patriotism, as well as abilities, of the very worthy people who are willing to die for freedom. But different men often see the same subject in different lights; and, therefore, I hope it will not be thought disrespectful to those people if, my opinions of a character very opposite to theirs, I shall speak my sentiments freely and without reserve or fear. This is no time for ceremony. The question before those who want their freedom is one of an awful moment in this country. For my own part, I consider it as nothing less than a question of freedom or slavery; and in proportion to the magnitude of the subject ought to be the freedom of the debate. It is only in this way that we can hope to arrive at the truth, and fulfill the great responsibility, which we hold

to our creator and our once free country. Should I keep back my opinions at such a time, through fear of giving offense, and I should consider myself as guilty of treason towards my Country as of an act of disloyalty toward the Majesty of Heaven, which I revere above all earthly kings? Nay say I. for the time to denounce the treason of those within our land is now!

Fellow citizens, it is natural to man to indulge in the illusions of hope. We are apt to shut our eyes against a painful truth, and listen to the song of that siren till she transforms us into beasts. Is this the part of wise men, engaged in a great and arduous struggle for liberty and freedom? Are we disposed to be of the numbers of those who, having eyes, see not, and, having ears, hear not, the things, which so nearly concern their temporal salvation? For my part, whatever anguish of spirit it may cost, I am willing to know the whole truth, to know the worst, and to provide for it and to expose it.

I have but one lamp by which my feet are guided, and that is the lamp of experience. I know of no way of judging of the future but by the past. And judging by the past, I wish to know what there has been in the conduct of the American Government for the last ten years to justify those hopes with which gentlemen of the House and Senate have been pleased to solace themselves in. Is it that insidious smile with which our petition has been lately received?

Trust it not, sir; it will prove a snare to your feet. Suffer not yourselves to be betrayed with a kiss. Ask yourselves how this gracious reception of our petition comports with those warlike preparations, which cover our waters and darken our land. Are our own fleets and armies necessary to a work of love and reconciliation? Have we shown ourselves so unwilling to be reconciled that force must be called in to win back our love? Let us not deceive ourselves, citizens of America. These are the implements of war and subjugation; the last arguments to which Dictators resort. I ask you citizens, what means is this martial array for, if its purpose be not to force us to submission? Can you assign any other possible motive for it? Has America any enemy, in this quarter of the world, to call for all this accumulation of navies and armies? No, Citizens, she has none. They are meant for us: they can be meant for no other. They are created to bind and rivet upon us those chains, which the American Government has been so long forging. And what have we to oppose to them? Shall we try argument? Good People, we have been trying that for the last ten years. Have we anything new to offer upon the subject? Nothing! We have held the subject up in every light of which it is capable; but it has been all in vain. Shall we resort to entreaty and humble supplication? What terms shall we find which have not been already exhausted? Let us not, I beseech you, free people, deceive ourselves. Citizens, we have done everything that could be done to avert the storm, which is now coming on. We have petitioned; we have remonstrated; we have supplicated; we have prostrated ourselves before the American throne, and have implored its interposition to arrest the tyrannical hands of the Government and its rogue agencies. Our petitions have been slighted; our remonstrances have produced additional violence and insult; our supplications have been disregarded; and we have been spurned, with contempt, from the foot of the government, which was created to protect us! In vain, after these things, may we indulge the fond hope of peace and reconciliation?

There is no longer any room for hope. If we wish to be free... if we mean to preserve inviolate those inestimable privileges for which we have been so long contending...if we mean not basely to abandon the noble struggle in which we have been so long engaged, and which we have pledged ourselves never to abandon until the glorious object of our contest shall be obtained...we must fight! I repeat it, free people, we must fight! An appeal to arms and to the God of hosts is all that is left us! They tell us, free people, that we are weak; unable to cope with so formidable an adversary. But when shall we be stronger? Will it be the next week, or the next year? Will it be when we are totally disarmed, and when an American guard shall be stationed in every house? Shall we gather strength by irresolution and inaction? Shall we acquire the means of effectual resistance by lying supinely on our backs and hugging the delusive phantom of hope, until our enemies shall have bound us hand and foot? Citizens, we are not weak if we make a proper use of those means, which the God of nature hath placed, in our power. The millions of people, armed in the holy cause of liberty and freedom, and in such a country as that which we possess, are invincible by any force, which our enemy can send against us. Besides, we shall not fight our battles alone. There is a just God who presides over the destinies of nations, and who will raise up friends to help fight our battles for us. The battle, my friends, is not to the strong alone; it is to the vigilant, the active, the brave. Besides, the citizens have no real elections or voice. If we were base enough to desire it, it is now too late to retire from the contest. There is no retreat but in submission and slavery! Our chains are forged! Their clanking may be heard on the plains of Boston and the cities of California! The war is inevitable...and let it come! I repeat it, let it come.

It is in vain, my free thinking friends, to extenuate the matter. Gentlemen may cry, Peace, Peace...but there is no peace. The war is actually begun! The next gale that sweeps will bring to our ears the clash of resounding arms! Our brethren are already in the field! Why stand we here idle? What is it that you citizens wish? What would you have? Is life so dear, or peace so sweet, as to be purchased at the price of chains and slavery? Forbid it, Almighty God! I know not what course others may take; but as for me, Give Me Liberty or Give Me Death!"

Do you have any idea where the bulk of this came from and who wrote it? If you do then you know it fits today just as it did when Patrick Henry spoke those words in 1775. I changed it to today's situation and replaced the King and England with America and the Government and it fits! The question is; will the American people cower and cave to total domination like the German, Russian, and Chinese's people did when their governments seized total power? Or will they fight once again like their forefathers did against insurmountable odds to regain their freedom? The Choice Is Yours! Freedom or Enslavement?

ABOUT THE AUTHOR

R.W. GLESS is the Author of "Thee Great American Illusion" Available at Amazon Books, Tower Book, Barns and Noble and other fine bookstores. He was also an elected official in California, an Investigative Reporter and Newspaper Publisher and a business owner entrepreneur, who also work for the Federal Government as an Independent Contractor.

* 9 7 8 1 5 0 0 7 1 6 6 0 8 *